# GAME CHANGER

How to take control and
increase your confidence,
personal power and
business success

## LINDA EVERETT

# RETHINK PRESS

First published in Great Britain 2015 by Rethink Press (www.rethinkpress.com)

To Matthew,
whose love and belief has been endless

# CONTENTS

# FOREWORD

When you look at your business or career – how do you feel? Is it all going according to plan? Do you face the future with the certain knowledge that you are firmly in the driving seat and have the confidence and self-belief to navigate any obstacle in your way? Is your life in perfect balance and are you happy, healthy and fulfilled? If so, then well done, you have successfully formulated the winning game plan. But for many people this is not the case; if you are one of them, the good news is that you are not alone … the great news is that you have picked up a copy of 'Game Changer.'

I met the author, Linda Everett, about 8 years ago. At the time, I was considering the possibility of launching my own company, but feeling unsure whether I had what it takes to succeed. You may not be thinking of such a drastic leap, but when you know that things can't continue as they are and you need to make some changes in order to feel happy and fulfilled, then you have to find a way to tap into the power within yourself. Game Changer helps you to do that, equipping you with the building blocks to recognise, embrace and create new opportunities and grow from life's challenges.

Since helping me find the courage, confidence and the inner power to strike out on my own, Linda has been my executive coach, mentor and professional sounding board. My company has gone from strength to strength, I am my own boss, in control of my own destiny and I have at long last found that elusive work/life balance without compromising my business' success.

So how did it happen? During my career I had learned many valuable skills, but I had also accumulated years of "conditioning";

beliefs about myself and my abilities that were shaped by the influence of others, from all areas of my life. Could I really run a successful company, as well as be a wife, mother, friend and daughter without running myself ragged each week? I had my doubts.

Such conditioning leads us to assess our expectations, abilities and chances of success in the light of who we perceive ourselves to be, rather than who we really are and what we might achieve. Even our thought patterns and behaviours can be counter-productive and limit our achievements and potential.

Linda helped me to fully recognise my strengths and stay focused on my goals, whilst challenging any conditioned beliefs that held no substance. Together, we developed a plan of action where all aspects of my business and personal life could be successfully managed and I still had time to take care of myself.

So what makes this book different to other personal development books? It is a book based on real life experience, not pseudo psychology or pretentious, academic platitudes. When I first read Linda's manuscript, I commented that I liked it because it was "real" – it is about real people dealing with real situations that we can all recognise – regardless of whether we are a business owner or trying to manage a career. Too many self-help books seem detached from reality and you don't get the feeling that the writer has ever experienced the same situations that you are trying to resolve. They advise others, but share nothing of themselves. By contrast, Linda shares her personal experiences illustrating how she has developed her own techniques to turn her own challenges, those of her immediate family and of course, her clients into success stories. This book is rich with everyday examples of the business and personal challenges that have been managed successfully by people like you and me.

So if you are ready to take that next step, to get into the driving seat and feel totally empowered to change the game, you need to read this book. Begin with the introduction. Your journey starts here.

Debbie Stenning<br>
CEO, Database Vision Ltd

# INTRODUCTION

Many people feel frustrated with the outcomes in their lives. They start out with a big vision for their business or career and the life they want to live, but soon discover that reality is very different. What's more, when faced with the challenges of that reality, fear of failure, rejection or loss prevents them from taking the action needed to achieve the outcome they want. Some hold back through lack of confidence or self-belief, and find reasons to stay as they are. Others need greater clarity, better direction or the right kind of support to help them reach their goals.

The never-ending demands of running a business or balancing a career whilst coping with the responsibilities and expectations that for many are part of modern life, make it seem easier for people to continue as they are, rather than focus on what they really want and how to make it happen. Valuable time and energy is invested in managing what they don't want, rather than in the actions they could take to reach their goals. The consequences have an impact on health, happiness and wellbeing, and result in lost business opportunities, wasted potential and everything in between.

The aim of this book is to provide a very different perspective, along with proven tools and strategies on how to increase your confidence, personal power and performance to drive your own professional success. Whether your ambition is to grow as a business or stand out and progress in your career, the same principles apply. They are based on almost 30 years of business and life experience and will change the way you think about yourself and what is possible.

1

It all begins with **vision** and being clear about what you want, so the steps you take move you forward in the direction that is truly right for you. **Self-mastery** raises your awareness of how you can build your personal power, because the right mindset is fundamental to your business and life success. Finally it addresses **performance**, with powerful insights that will change the way you see yourself and how you feel. If you are serious about success and committed to being your best self, you can transform your results. The examples I share are true stories of inspiring people I have had the privilege of working with, although to protect their privacy, their names have been changed.

I hope this book will inspire and empower you to take control of your business, your career or any part of your life that is not delivering the outcomes you want. Be the game changer in your own life, because it's not lack of talent, ability or desire for success that limits potential. It is that few of us start out with the mindset we need to achieve our goals and most of us spend our lives giving away our power.

By changing the way you think and becoming more strategic in your approach, you will develop a more focused and empowered perspective. Seemingly impossible challenges, or circumstances beyond your control become manageable as you see a way forward.

My own early experiences of powerlessness and frustration made me acutely aware that not everyone thinks and behaves in the same way. Attitudes and beliefs that influence behaviour are often passed down through the generations, affecting the outcomes and potential of those who follow. Whilst many of these influences are helpful and supportive, others are less so and if as adults we accept them without challenge, they continue to limit our potential.

As I sought answers to change the outcomes in my own life, I made a remarkable discovery. What I learnt helped me to build a successful business – beyond anything I could have imagined – and discover talents I had no idea I possessed. For the first time, I realised the power I had to change my outcomes.

Years later, faced with some truly life-changing experiences, I came to fully understand the importance and need to feel empowered, not only to achieve our professional goals, but to make better choices in all areas of our lives so we can transform the outcomes.

The adventure starts the moment you decide to take control. Whether you have ambitious business or career goals, a personal vision for yourself, or are unhappy with your life and want to make some changes, this book will inspire and show you how to step up, reclaim your power and start changing the game.

# Part One

# VISION

# One

# KNOW YOUR OUTCOME

Sometimes, the least likely encounters in our lives are the most significant. Mine was, of all places, at a Sunday morning football match in the early 1980s. It introduced me to the world of direct sales cosmetics and business ownership. I had never heard of Jafra before, but I was familiar with the parent company Gillette and with some persuasion, I agreed to try the products. A week later, I was impressed enough to sign as a consultant. As I handed over my £10 deposit and parted with all the money I had to live on until the end of the month, I took a leap of faith that I'd find a way to pay the balance. In those days, I didn't drive and I had no clear idea where to begin, but I believed passionately that women should take care of themselves and good skincare is essential. With such an impressive product, I knew it was an opportunity I had to take, though I had no idea where it would lead. My only thoughts were to get started. If I allowed myself to panic, I would struggle, so I began to think 'How can I…?'

This became my mantra.

The first few weeks in the business were tough, but I made myself learn from every knock-back or mistake and just kept going. Small successes grew into bigger ones and the more I succeeded, the further I challenged myself. As time went by, I stopped wondering whether the big goals were achievable. Instead, I focused on how I could make it happen. Not exactly a *business* plan, more of an *action* plan. When something didn't work, I tried a different approach until I got there.

It was scary and exhilarating at the same time and it taught me a great deal about resilience, personal power and what can be achieved with the right mindset.

> *'The question isn't Who is going to let me; it's Who is going to stop me?'*
>
> AYN RAND

So think about your goal. Give it shape and write it down. How important is it to you? Is it a 'nice to have' or a 'must'? Be honest with yourself, even if it seems impossible to achieve and your negative self-talk is kicking in as you read. When you are clear that this is something you really want, focus on all the possible ways to get there, not just the most obvious or familiar. Aim to come up with ideas you can explore and develop, without pre-judging whether they will work. The big question you need to ask is:

**Q.** 'What could I try?'

One of the things I discovered as I went through this process is that once you make a commitment to take action, you need to be held accountable for what you say you will do. Accountability works because if you are serious about your goal, the fear of not trying and how that would make you feel about yourself is a greater motivator than any fear of failure. In my case, I knew that if I failed I could learn from the experience and try again, but not to try would change the way I saw myself. This powerful insight increased my resourcefulness and determination to succeed. As long as I was committed, there was always a way forward.

This discovery was truly transformational for my business. I realised that talent and ability are rarely the reasons that define success. Many people have both. What matters is the way you think and whether you allow thoughts or past experiences to limit you. Focusing on the problem only keeps you stuck in negativity. It wastes your time, drains your mental and physical energy and brings you down. In no time at all, you are reminding yourself of countless reasons why 'nothing will ever change', why 'you're not up to the challenge', why 'you're not good enough', etc., etc., Refuse to do that to yourself, or allow anyone else to do it to you, ever again. It is the fastest way to sabotage your goals and dreams.

Your real power lies in the choices you make and those choices are formed by the way you think. In that moment of clarity, everything changes. Regardless of any obstacles you currently face, or how insurmountable they seem, you always have a choice. Focus on what you really want, and keep it at the forefront of your mind. Your vision of success will shape the choices you make and the outcomes you achieve beyond any you can imagine.

If life has a habit of throwing you curve balls, or people are quick to tell you something cannot be done, it is always up to you to decide what you accept and how you respond. Until now, you may not have realised you have a choice (It took me many years), or understood that your thoughts either support or undermine your success. Perhaps you've been taught that somehow everything will work out and success will naturally come your way. I used to think so too, heavily influenced by Hollywood movies as a child and brought up with the mistaken belief that being good was enough. I learnt very quickly that it's not. Life doesn't work that way.

In the real world, if you sit back waiting patiently for recognition, reward or success, you will be passed by. If you are truly serious about achieving your goals and making your vision of success happen, you need to be in the driving seat. The time has come to step up, so focus on the outcome you want, change the questions you ask and start defining success on your own terms. From the moment you make that commitment, nothing will ever be the same again.

> *'It is not possible to solve a problem*
> *within the same consciousness*
> *that produced it.'*
>
> ALBERT EINSTEIN

One of the challenges you face is maintaining the belief that you are good enough for the role you want, whether that's as CEO of your own company or a scary but oh-so-exciting career opportunity that you would love to be offered. Being good enough is a belief based on where you are now, rather than who you will become, as you move forward and grow into the role. Refuse to pre-judge your potential. Instead, invest your energy into being the best you can be and make every day count. Don't wait for the time to be right. Focus on your vision of success, identify the skills, strategies and mindset you need to get you there and start walking the talk. As your confidence increases, so will your self-belief.

Three months after I began working for Jafra, I was invited to a regional lunch. I watched in amazement as countless women stepped up to receive recognition and further rewards for all they had achieved. Towards the end, a handful of newly-appointed managers were called out and presented with a briefcase and scarf. In a defining moment, I knew without a shadow of doubt that next time around, I would be one of them.

What I hadn't allowed for though, was the discovery that I was pregnant. After an earlier miscarriage, I was naturally elated by the news, but I also realised that if I was going to achieve my management goal, I had limited time before my baby was born. That realisation gave me the impetus I needed to focus on building a team. My enthusiasm and excitement seemed to rub off on others, because that first team quickly developed and became two, considerably raising my profile within the company. Just before my son's birth, I received that briefcase and scarf, along with the grand title of Zone Manager. My lineage, in more ways than one, was growing fast.

Over the following nine years, my business went from strength to strength, developing into nine branches throughout the South East and far exceeding anything I could have imagined. During that time I learnt much about business and how to develop potential that is too often wasted through lack of confidence, the right kind of support or a clear direction. Most of all, I became fascinated by the link between empowerment and the realisation of potential.

It really helps to know what you want, yet sometimes the catalyst for change is to identify what you *don't* want. If your vision of success is still unclear, think about what is important to you and how that affects the way you run your business, perform in your career or manage your personal life? How is it demonstrated in the behaviour, expectations and results you or others deliver?

Consciously or not, values play a significant role in the ethos of any company. They influence what is delivered and how people perform, providing a framework, a set of expectations of what the business owner or company considers important. Being clear about your own values can help you make better decisions and experience less stress. Unfortunately, much of the conflict we experience in life is value-related. Over time, you realise that like-minded clients are easier to attract and retain. You find you enjoy doing business with them, rather than with those who drain your energy.

Think about what you are known for, or how you want to be seen. Identify what is important to you as a customer. What makes the difference and ensures you go back for more? Why do you naturally recommend some people or places, but not others? What is it that makes them excel and stand out from the rest?

## Exercise

Identify and write down the 10-15 most important values to you in life. Think about what you must have, whether professionally or personally, to be happy.

Examples of values you could choose from include: trust, respect, achievement, integrity, independence, health, friendship, humour, adventure, communication, personal growth and freedom.

Now decide on your top ten most important values and rank them in order of importance.

Creating a compelling vision of what you want to achieve, is often a process that evolves over time. It cannot be someone else's idea of success. This is your vision, based on your values and what success means to you. Whether professionally or personally, being clear about what you want to achieve will shape the choices you make and the direction you take. Currently, there may be pieces missing, but as you read on and listen to your heart, your vision will take shape. With clarity, you can begin to take action and start turning your vision into reality.

*'Find the courage to live the life of your own dreams... The rest will take care of itself.'*

OPRAH WINFREY

# Two

# WHAT DRIVES YOU?

Success can be achieved in any area of life, if you are determined and stay focused on your goal. The right mindset and a clear determination to succeed is an unstoppable force. At the very point when your goals become a must, rather than a 'nice to have', everything begins to change. You start taking your own performance seriously… and so does everyone else. If past experiences have held you back, or lack of support has undermined your confidence, turn a fresh page and begin anew. Learn from what has gone before and use it to inspire you to achieve the outcomes you want.

> *'People don't buy what you do. They buy why you do it.'*
>
> SIMON SINEK

There are two important questions you need to be able to answer, if you want to increase your business or career momentum: 'What drives you?' and 'Why is it important to you to turn your vision into reality?'

Your reasons will fuel the energy and passion that you invest in achieving your goals. They are the motivation behind your desire for success, the attraction factor people buy into and the power surge that drives action. They are your 'Why?'

Most of us would enjoy a higher income, yet it's rare that money alone is the driving force behind a desire for success. Unless you are driven to accumulate wealth for its own sake, money is no more than a resource that gives you greater choice in life. So what inspires you? What is it about what you do, or want to do that drives you on? What gives your business or career meaning and purpose, shaping the actions you take and your direction of travel? The answers to these questions reveal the personal reasons behind what drives you. They bring emotion and depth to your vision of success.

Whatever the story behind your 'why', you have given it meaning and purpose. Write it down. It will be a powerful reminder when times get tough and you begin to doubt yourself. The real challenge is not your ability to achieve your goals, but how determined you are to find a way. If you have a big enough reason for success, you feel empowered to make it happen.

> *'Man is so made that when anything fires his soul, impossibilities vanish.'*
>
> JEAN DE LA FONTAINE

A few hours after my son was born, he developed a heart condition and spent the first week of his life in the special care baby unit (SCBU) of my local hospital. Fortunately, he had excellent care and the problem was identified and treated quickly with no lasting effects, but it was a traumatic time. Some years later, my local paper ran a front-page story highlighting the terrible dilemma the SCBU faced, if a second baby was taken ill. There was a dire need for another piece of specialist equipment, but the cost at that time, was a prohibitive £9,000.

As I read the headline, my first thought was 'Someone should do something', before it struck me that I had a very powerful reason to act. That realisation led me to begin a fundraising campaign that reached out to businesses, families and individuals who either lived in the town, or worked in the community. It wasn't easy with a business to run and a young family, but I had to do it. This was a debt I wanted to repay and failure was not an option. I had no previous fundraising experience, but I did have a great deal of persistence and determination, so I drew up a plan and the campaign took off. As word spread, people came from many different directions to help or contribute, until raising the money gained a momentum of its own. In those pre-internet times, we relied on word of mouth, but it worked. Within three months, the money was raised.

> *'Your vision will become clear only when you can look into your own heart. Who looks outside, dreams; who looks inside, awakens.'*
>
> CARL JUNG

So what does success look like to you? How would you feel if you could achieve what you want and reach your goals? What difference would that make to you and the life you want? Close your eyes and allow yourself to imagine. What if…?

Now hold on to that vision and imagine you had the courage to make your professional and personal life work on your terms, shaping the direction you take and the decisions you make. How might that change the way you feel about yourself and the actions you take, right now? How would it influence the choices you make and the person you would become in the process?

A new client was deeply unhappy that a young, talented graduate colleague had been fast-tracked into a role that had taken her many years to reach. My client had more experience, but struggled to communicate effectively and promote herself well. She was considering applying for a promotion that would have placed her in direct competition with her colleague. Already stressed, she described the role as more demanding, with longer hours and the potential for weekend work. I asked her why she was considering the role. She replied that she didn't enjoy her current role and wanted to progress her career, but felt that she was being overlooked. This completely changed the picture.

We began by identifying her strengths and talents, and improving her communication and presentation skills within her current role. Working to her strengths, her confidence increased and she became more effective, raising her profile within the department. She was also more proactive at meetings, consciously demonstrating her knowledge and insight through her contributions and actions. It paid off. In the next round of departmental changes, she was offered a new and more senior role that suited her perfectly.

Your vision of success has to align with what really matters to you and what is important in the wider context of your life. These same principles applied to your business or career help you to make better decisions about the outcomes you want. By seeing yourself as CEO (Chief Executive Officer) of your business, or your own personal career manager, you change the context. When you see the big picture of the choices you make, it's easier to identify the detail of how you are going to achieve your goals. Such clarity offers a compass to guide your actions and help you stay on course.

*'So many of our dreams at first
seem impossible, then they seem
improbable, and then when we
summon the will, they soon
become inevitable.'*

CHRISTOPHER REEVE

_____

Knowing what you want and why it's important to you is truly powerful. It is as though destiny has called. You have found your purpose. When that happens, you start defining success on your own terms and shaping your own direction, rather than following everyone else. You have a clear sense of purpose. Your personal power increases and everything in your life begins to change.

# Three

## THE BIG PICTURE

We are the sum total of all that we are and have experienced in our lives. We bring our whole selves into everything we do, so what goes on in any one area has an impact on our performance in the rest. It is not possible to separate the personal from our professional life completely, regardless of how we may try, so to achieve our vision of success we need a holistic approach.

In the past, men left the house every day, free to focus on their careers, in effect compartmentalising their lives. They were confident in the knowledge there was a woman at home to deal with family life and anything considered domestic. Personal events or family concerns still had an impact, but there was less expectation for men to become involved because work and family domains were separate and clearly defined.

Now those domains are shared and women especially find themselves with a different set of challenges to overcome. Conditioned to be the caregivers for everyone, they generally still bear the lion's share of responsibility for the family, regardless of help from a supportive partner. It's a tough habit to break, and the pressure can be immense.

So developing a broader definition of success, and making it part of your vision for your business, means becoming more aware of the big picture and including your own needs in the equation. If you want to perform at your best, how you travel is as important as the destination. It is essential to find a way to make your life and business work for you, and to listen to what you need. As CEO, you are responsible for your own wellbeing and it's within your power to create a successful, happy and fulfilling life.

In striving to achieve success in business, look at your life as a whole. How well you perform is the key to your achievement, so take care of you first, not last. If that makes you uncomfortable, it is probably because this is an unfamiliar concept. Try thinking of it as being self-full, not self-ish. Taking care of your health and wellbeing really does pay off. It means you have the energy and vitality to cope with the many demands and expectations to come. If you neglect yourself, everything and everyone who relies on you is affected. For me it's a question of logic.

> ## 'Happiness is not a destination,
> ## it's a way of travelling.'
> ROBERT HOLDEN

Any part of your life has the power to positively influence, or deeply undermine your success, if it is taken for granted. In a later chapter, we will look at energy drainers, but for now it's enough to know that no matter how focused you are on your goals, the unexpected can and does happen. By taking control and creating a more balanced life, you build your success on strong foundations.

So what does balance mean? In practice, it means looking at your life as a whole and addressing all aspects. It means making time to plan, so that you not only become more effective in the way you manage your time and commitments, but you ensure your own needs are met too.

Rather than endless To Do lists, try creating a power plan for the week ahead. Power planning includes the detail that makes your whole life work, not just the business. It looks at weekly ongoing commitments such as the need to organise meals, prepare clothes, do the grocery shop and household chores. It sets time aside to exercise, for family and friends, or just to do those things that are important to you. Begin by allocating realistic time frames to all tasks, or give them pockets of time until the task is complete. Manage expectations and be willing to delegate or share the load. Making time for yourself is important. It feeds the spirit and helps you perform at your best. Reading a great book, listening to music, going for a walk or making time to dance… these are all small ways to make a difference to your quality of life, so stop making excuses and take control. This is non-negotiable. Your challenge is to find a way, so change your mindset and start thinking 'How can I?'

Suzanne, one of my clients, loved to run, but began to feel guilty every time she prepared to do so, because her husband wanted her to spend time with him and come to the pub instead. It started to cause resentment.

I asked her how important running was to her.

'It makes me feel alive,' she answered. 'When I don't run, I feel like something is missing in my life.'

Clearly, running was something that Suzanne needed to do, to feed her spirit. She saw it as essential to her happiness and wellbeing, but also recognised that time with her husband mattered too.

We discussed her options and identified that the real issue was the lack of planning and poor communication. By being more organised and planning ahead, Susanne saw a way she could make time for her running and still be free to go out with her husband. When she told him how she felt and shared her plan, Suzanne's husband understood and became very supportive.

A life out of balance, no matter how successful it appears on the surface, brings consequences. In the short term, most people cope, but when the imbalance becomes a way of life, it really doesn't work.

Lack of balance has the power to affect quality of life, health and wellbeing, relationships and business performance. You are left feeling tired, stressed and unhappy, rather than strong, confident and empowered. If you allow yourself to reach this point, you are at your most vulnerable. It's when the goalposts can change in an instant, leaving you forced to make radical changes to your life.

I learnt this lesson many years ago in my Jafra days. Success in our professional lives, unless well managed, can make huge demands on our time. With a very young family and a business to run from home without the safety net of office hours, I found myself pulled in many directions. When I had got to the stage of truly wondering how I was going to get through the week ahead, my back seized up and I couldn't move. My body had found a way to get my attention and make sure I listened. I no longer had a choice and I learnt that my world didn't end just because I couldn't meet its demands. Instead, over the next couple of weeks, I had plenty of time to plan the changes I needed to make in my life.

It's important to understand that none of us are one-dimensional. We perform best when our needs are met, when we're happy and can live a balanced and fulfilling life. Of course, there are times when we're under pressure and our priorities have to change, but in the long term, that is not a sustainable way to live or to run a business. There are always consequences.

Our willingness to see our lives as a whole allows us to recognise what we need and decide how to make daily life work. A quick SWOT analysis (Strengths, Weaknesses, Opportunities and Threats) will show up any imbalances that need to be addressed, before they become problematic.

Taking control is a choice. It undoubtedly challenges you, but the more you do it, the stronger and more effective you become. Most of all, you feel empowered to create the life you want, through the choices you make.

# Four

## KNOW YOUR WORTH

I didn't start out with a carefully-designed career plan. For years I wondered what was wrong with me. Every time I mastered a challenge or developed a new skill, I found it wasn't enough. No matter how much I enjoyed the learning or how enthused I was with the subject, I was always left with unanswered questions and a desire for something more. This happened many times and each discovery took me in a new direction, or so it seemed. Then one day, something happened that triggered a light bulb moment. I suddenly realised my interest in these many directions resembled pieces of a jigsaw puzzle. Separately, they were different skills, talents and abilities, but when pieced together, they gave shape to a whole new picture. My skills were transferable and just as relevant in this new context. That realisation left me with an empowering visual image. Every piece of the jigsaw was part of a unique personal story that had meaning and purpose. It made complete sense.

When you recognise the extent of what you have to offer, it is much easier to share that knowledge with others, whether you are growing your business or building a career. Shared experiences or common interests break down barriers and frequently lead to new opportunities, which is why some people do business on a golf course. We take so many of our skills, personal qualities and accomplishments for granted, yet they offer great insight into who we are and what we have to offer, not just what we do. In business, people want to know why they should choose you. What is it that makes you special, unique or different from all the rest? Your picture tells that story.

# Exercise

- Identify the skills, strengths, qualities and abilities that make up the pieces in your jigsaw puzzle. Create a picture of who you **are**, not just what you **do**.
- Include your values, the things you are passionate about and what you most enjoy.
- Use this as a work in progress, to help you shape the direction of your life and your vision of success.

The beauty of the jigsaw analogy is that you can include your successes and experiences along with any defining moments. Its purpose is to provide you with an empowering visual image of what makes you unique, what you have to offer and bring clarity to your vision of what you want. I've had many defining moments in my life. I see them as forks in the road. This is the one that gave shape to my jigsaw picture and led me to train formally as a coach.

In the late 90s, whilst in my local library doing some business research on the Internet, I came across a detailed description of coaching. In that moment, all the lights in my world lit up. I felt as though I was reading a definition of myself that I had never seen before and wondered how I could have missed something so obvious. Immediately, I saw the connection between everything I had ever done. Like a mind-map, it gave new meaning to my interest in the psychology of performance and the decade I had spent studying it. I remembered the questions I'd been compelled to raise about self-image when I trained as an Image consultant. It brought together my professional background and business expertise and the many difficult and challenging life experiences where I'd felt sorely tested and questioned 'why?' I also realised why the impact of the recession had so profoundly influenced my thoughts around self-image and its power to influence and shape the choices we make. Suddenly, everything came together and fell into place. In that moment, it seemed to me that I'd been preparing for this all my life.

> *'We are what we think. All that we are arises with our thoughts. With our thoughts, we make our world.'*
>
> BUDDHA

In 1991, the recession that decimated the construction industry left my husband unemployed after 19 years in architecture. Only two years earlier, he had been offered five jobs in one week, so it was quite a shock. His high-profile company went from renting four floors with 600 employees to just one with 60 people, all within six months. For all my husband's talent and considerable experience, he was out of work for two and a half years.

During that time, I learnt much about the way people define themselves and others: by what they do for a living. Many of those (at that time, mainly professional men) who had been made redundant or were unable to find work, described themselves as 'nothing' without a job. They felt powerless and worthless in the face of a situation that many had never experienced before in their lives. It was such a disempowering definition for anyone to live with that it wasn't surprising to read that some professional men chose to commit suicide. My husband told me of others he met who continued to put on a suit every day, pretending to their wives they still had a job.

Work is one of the ways people gain status and identity. If they have invested years of their life in building that identity, only to find it lost through circumstances beyond their control, it is understandable that they feel they have lost themselves. The consequences can be anything from a ripple effect to a tidal wave on their lives and self-esteem.

In this sense, there were similarities with the middle class Bosnian refugee family with whom I worked as a volunteer at that time. Like many others, they had lost everything familiar to them – their home, two businesses, a lifetime of accumulated belongings, their community and even their country. Before the war, these things had defined who they were, providing them with an identity and status. In their new and very different circumstances, this family and many more throughout the world have to rediscover themselves.

Life presents us with many challenges that can truly undermine our sense of self and our confidence and belief in the future. Without a strong foundation grounded in who we are, we lack clarity and direction. Relationship break-ups, unemployment, health issues and even the process of growing older in the modern world all have the potential to be hugely damaging to self-esteem and our ability to recover and thrive. The recognition that you have the power to choose your response no matter what, prevents you from being a victim of your life. Stress is reduced by the act of taking control, and the more you do it, the more resilient and empowered you become.

When the enormity of our situation became clear, my mindset changed. Everything I had learnt and experienced up to that moment came to the fore, with a need to not only survive but to find a way to manage the endless daily stress of uncertainty, as we waited for each day's post. My priority was our family's health and wellbeing, so I decided to start growing organic fruit and vegetables and baking bread. Through trial and error and with a great deal of help from the local library, we transformed our quality of life, giving it new meaning and purpose.

After a year out of work, my husband became eligible for an executive job club, which gave him access to three months of open learning at the local Further and Advanced Education College. I encouraged him to make good use of it and see it as an opportunity to gain valuable CAD experience and qualifications previously denied to him when in work. I believed that when the market picked up, this new skill would increase his worth. That proved to be the case, yet of those who attended the course, most wasted the opportunity.

> *'Your living is determined not so much by what life brings you as by the attitude you bring to life; not so much by what happens to you as by the way your mind looks at what happens.'*
>
> LEWIS L. DUNNINGTON

When you define yourself by who you are, rather than what you have, your value and personal power comes from within. Those things can never be lost. You can take them into any situation, apply them to any circumstance and they will support you throughout your life, regardless of age, external pressures or challenges. Refuse to give away your power or allow yourself to feel like a victim of circumstance, no matter what you experience. Instead, take control of your own life and discover what is possible. Personal power is a choice.

# Five

## STAND OUT

To succeed in this globally competitive market, you must have a clear definition of what you have to offer and a compelling vision of what you want to achieve, whether you are running a business or building your career. Expectations are high so you must stand out. That requires confidence and a willingness to drive and embrace new opportunities. Every experience or challenge offers scope to raise your profile and find out how far you can go.

You may want to be known as an expert in your field or to become the go-to person in your industry. Consider ways you can demonstrate thought leadership and in the process, drive your own success, based on the height of the bar you set for yourself. There are no short cuts to expertise. You need to do the work and build a strong foundation of knowledge, skills and experience for credibility. Opportunities provide the stepping-stones to help us stand out.

*'Circumstances may cause interruptions and delays, but never lose sight of your goal. Prepare yourself in every way you can by increasing your knowledge and adding to your experience, so that you can make the most of opportunity when it occurs.'*

MARIO ANDRETTI

So find your passion. What drives you to do what you do? Think about what makes you different. Why should people invest in you, rather than someone else equally hungry for their business? Consider what you can offer to grab their attention and make them want to buy. Know what is really important to the audience you want to reach.

If you can identify what that is and massively exceed their expectations, not only will you get their business, you will keep it. Clients and contacts will be happy to share their knowledge and experience of working with you as they recommend you to others. You will be seen as the go-to person in your field, inspiring confidence, trust and credibility. This is invaluable. It builds your reputation and broadens your reach. With greater awareness of what makes you different, special, or unique in your field, you can develop and market yourself effectively, promoting those differences as part of your brand. Not only will this help you stand out, it allows you to charge more for your service and skills.

The values that define your business and the way you are seen professionally are really important. They represent your identity in the business world: your brand. Values embody what you stand for, so they need to be reflected in everything you do. That identity is what people buy into. Wherever there is a conflict of values, there are always problems. So become clear about your values, what you stand for and what people can expect if they choose to work with you. This will increase your credibility. By being congruent in all that you do, you will stand out from the rest.

During my years with Jafra, I came to realise the value and importance of excellent customer service. In the beginning, it wasn't something I particularly thought about. I just treated people the way I wanted to be treated. For me, that meant being authentic, reliable and always keeping my word. It meant communicating clearly and effectively, and ensuring my clients felt valued. I'd had many experiences when sales people were only interested in how much money they could make, rather than genuinely wanting to help solve a problem. I had also known people who went the extra mile to provide outstanding customer service and they were the ones who got my business.

Such experiences shaped my attitude when dealing with my own clients. I wanted to provide the kind of service that gave people a superb support system, made their lives easier and delivered outstanding results. I also wanted them to know they mattered and that my approach was not dependent on how much money they spent, as so often happens. I soon discovered that this personal approach to customer service worked. In addition to their regular orders, clients were buying new products over the phone purely on my recommendation.

> *'All of the top achievers I know are life-long learners, looking for new skills, insights, and ideas. If they're not learning, they're not growing and not moving toward excellence.'*
>
> DENIS WAITLEY

Any significant success in your business or career depends on what sets you apart from everyone else, and how well you meet the needs of the people who invest in you. At that time, the direct sales cosmetics industry was renowned for one-off purchases that left clients with nowhere to go for a replacement, or any way to add to their range. That reputation almost deterred me from signing with the company. I saw the importance of building longer-term relationships with people, regardless of the number of products they initially bought at my classes. It was a logic that helped my business stand out. Although not part of the company's training, my follow-up calls were well received and to my surprise, generated further sales and new bookings. This not only increased my monthly income, but many clients continued to order from me regularly throughout all of the following nine years. Their initial investment may have been quite modest, but their long-term value to my business was considerable.

> *'No one ever attains very eminent success by simply doing what is required of him; it is the amount and excellence of what is over and above the required that determines the greatness of ultimate distinction.'*
>
> CHARLES KENDALL ADAMS

Building long-term relationships founded on genuine commitment and trust is fundamental to business growth and your vision of success. When people invest their trust in you, they put their reputation and judgement on the line – something rarely realised and often taken for granted. Ensuring people feel valued is a responsibility, but it also provides you with a wonderful opportunity to stand out, regardless of your field of expertise.

Of course, success can bring its own challenges. People who exceed expectations generally find themselves in great demand. As the benefits and opportunities increase, so too does the pressure. Professional demands can take over and throw your life out of balance, so you must take control from the outset.

A client who found herself in this situation felt she had no alternative but to reschedule some of her confirmed business commitments, after one of her clients had an emergency and needed her to travel to their office. Whilst happy to do this, re-scheduling at short notice had the potential to jeopardise relationships with other clients. It also allowed her business commitments to be controlled by the needs of just one. I suggested she negotiate her availability with the client by asking for a private room to be made available to her where she could make her scheduled calls, yet still be on site to support her client through their emergency. They were more than happy to comply.

Focus on your client's needs and look at how you can align them with your own to create a win/win outcome. Think creatively. If you don't take control of your business or role and deliver on your own terms, you risk overload or burnout. You need to be in control of your business, not to be controlled by its demands. How you respond to these challenges will either diminish or increase your personal power, confidence and self-image. As CEO of your business, taking control and finding a way to achieve win/win outcomes, demonstrates authority and helps you stand out from the rest.

# Six

# RAISE YOUR PROFILE

Success is rarely achieved in isolation. Whatever your goals in life, you need other people to help make them happen. People provide us with help, support and inspiration. They offer all kinds of opportunities we may never have considered or known about. They have connections, experiences and ideas of their own, like the wonderful taxi driver who was curious when I asked him to take me to my local hospital's Special Care Baby Unit. I explained that I had recently begun a town-wide fundraising drive to buy a piece of specialised equipment for the unit. He was delighted. Two days earlier, the local taxi driving community, of which he was a committee member, had organised a social evening, raising hundreds of pounds for charity. They were looking for a suitable cause to donate the money to.

Raising your profile means opening yourself up to new possibilities and the chance to create different outcomes. It's a way to let other people know you're out there. If what you have to offer happens to match what someone else is looking for, there's an affinity. Meeting that cab driver was serendipity and became a win/win opportunity for us both ... and of course, the SCBU.

I've seen this work many times, both professionally and on a personal level.

The first time it happened in my business was by chance. Some months after my son was born, I was busy preparing for my cosmetics class later that evening. The Christmas gift range had arrived and I was pondering how I was going to carry everything. Along with my case of products and support items for the class, I had all the new gifts, my Christmas display materials and a bag of polystyrene chippings (representing snow).

As I sat there, feeling rather daunted, I had an idea. I could use my big, round wicker baby basket to carry the Christmas gifts. Unfortunately, because of its shape, the items didn't sit well in the basket, so I tried setting them on a base of the chippings. Effective, but rather dull and unattractive. Hmmm… I tried covering the chippings with a square of plain red satin, re-positioned the gift items and suddenly, the basket took on life. A long red ribbon wound to cover the handle and finished on either side with two big bows, some silver tinsel around the edge and wow. I had a portable Christmas display unit that looked fantastic.

At my class, the Christmas basket was passed around with enthusiasm. Everyone wanted to buy. I was invited to bring it along to the next management meeting, which coincided with the town's market day. As I carefully carried the basket through the street *en route* from the car park, people actually stopped me. They wanted to know what I was selling and if the gifts on display were for sale. This generated more business and new, unexpected leads.

More was to come. Following the management meeting, my Christmas basket idea was shared with Jafra International's Head Office and adopted by consultants and managers throughout the whole of the UK and Northern Ireland. I'd unwittingly raised my profile by doing something innovative to solve a problem and it had opened doors. I had new business, new leads and had suddenly become someone to watch within the organisation.

I share this story because when you change the way you think, you change your outcomes. If your focus is on finding solutions rather than being caught up in the problem, you have a different approach.

It not only gets results, it gets you noticed. People will respond to what you're doing because it inspires them and makes them want to engage, but first they have to know you are out there.

> *'Believe in yourself and there will come a day when others will have no choice but to believe in you.'*
>
> CYNTHIA KERSEY

One of the reasons for the success of social media is that it allows immediate access to a wider circle of people and an opportunity to engage. Of course, you have to learn how to use it wisely, but social media is a powerful way you can transform your business reach and build relationships that were once thought impossible. It can also help you gain a reputation as an expert in your field. That requires effort and commitment, but it can be done. Once you have a clear vision of what you want to achieve, it is easy to see how developing your skills in public speaking, social media or even professional writing can be valuable additions in your pursuit of greater success.

The clearer you are about what you want, and can describe in detail your vision of success, the easier it is to design a plan and take action. As you progress, you'll attract people and opportunities that will support you in turning your vision into reality. You'll have a clear direction and will project the certainty of purpose and confidence you need, to inspire others to follow your lead.

Don't wait until you know more or have achieved greater success. Begin now. Set your own bar high and live up to it. Use it as your guide in everything you do. Your reputation will grow with you. We don't always realise the impact we have on others, or how our vision of what's possible resonates with someone else. They may be waiting in the wings until the right combination of circumstance, brings them forward. In the meantime, your passion, commitment and determination will inspire confidence and reinforce belief in your expertise. The more you stand out, the greater the challenges and opportunities you will attract, but stay true to your vision and focus on the direction you want to take. This is your journey and you have it within your power to shape its direction.

## Exercise

**Q.** To progress your business or professional role, who do you want or need to gain access to and why? Be as specific as you can.

**Q.** How could that help you with your business or professional role? Think of all the present and future possibilities you can.

**Q.** What specific actions could you take to build those contacts and who do you know who might help?

Ideally, you need to develop a number of approaches and cover different angles. Writing is one option. Developing a series of blogs or White Papers can demonstrate your knowledge and expertise. Getting a book published, or finding a way to write for a professional magazine, increases credibility and reaches a wider audience. YouTube videos, podcasts, public speaking opportunities or taking part in events are further ways of raising your profile.

People are always looking for those who are passionate about what they do and can demonstrate expertise, so you need to find a way to let them know you're out there by raising your profile and being open to opportunity.

Soon after I set up my coaching practice, I took part in a high profile event that was open to the general public. It attracted thousands of people and led to a significant number of new clients. One of the attendees I met there was the events manager for a large country club. She invited me to be a future guest speaker at a regular lunchtime event. That opportunity introduced me to another new client and an invitation to write for a local magazine.

Raising your profile lets people know you are out there. If you do it well, people remember you. It sows a seed. It also demonstrates confidence and attracts opportunities that can further your success. Start planning now, so that when you are ready, you have strategies in place that will get you noticed.

# Seven

# YOUR CIRCLE OF INFLUENCE

Too often, we fail to see the opportunities available to us. Your success will be as much to do with your ability to think differently and recognise new opportunities as it will your talent and skills, regardless of how good you are.

## Exercise

You already have a circle of influence that could help you. Here are some ideas to make you think. List all of the following:

- People you already know, either professionally or personally
- People you have lost touch with
- People you used to work with or met through business
- People from school, college or university
- People from groups or clubs you belong to, or used to know
- People from your church, either past or present
- Neighbours past and present
- People who provide a service to you, like your hairdresser, car mechanic or personal trainer
- Family and friends

- Friends of family and friends
- Your contacts through social media

In fact, everyone you have ever met or engaged with has the potential to be part of your contacts list. Even if you only reconnect with a few, you have massively broadened your circle of influence. Social media and Google make it easy to find people you've lost touch with, so send a personal message, reconnect and renew those relationships. Think of it as an opportunity to expand your circle of influence.

> *'Don't wait for opportunity to come knocking on your door. Go out and give it directions.'*
>
> ANON

Your connections are a valuable resource. If you have a niche market in a specific background, you have access to a great many skilled, talented and knowledgeable contacts you have made along the way. It is easy to forget that the people you once knew as friends have moved forward and made connections in their lives too. These are people you knew through sport or the dances you went to. They're students you studied with, or colleagues you worked alongside. There are countless people who have gone on to build lives, businesses or careers since you were last in touch and it's likely they will be delighted to hear from you, if you show a genuine interest in renewing the relationship.

I went through this process with a new client who had set up her own research business and needed to develop her circle of influence. She was amazed to discover that she had a long list of high profile academics and scientists who previously she had only ever thought of as friends.

If you are in business or you network regularly, you will invariably meet new people who become part of your circle of influence. Many will hand over a business card, but surprisingly few know how to network effectively and take the time to follow up in a positive and authentic way. This means not just blatantly trying to sell their product or service to you, or automatically adding your name to their mailing list without your agreement.

The best kind of networking aims to build relationships by being genuinely interested in other people and making time to get to know them. When that happens, it is only natural that they are happy to reciprocate. With so few people making real and meaningful connections with others, your phone call or personalised email will speak volumes. Follow it up with an invite to meet for coffee and keep the arrangement. Within that meeting is a seed of opportunity for both of you, if you look for it.

With Jafra Cosmetics, whenever I had a promotion to work for, I had to plan how I was going to achieve it. I didn't have the time to leave it to chance, so I learnt how to ask for help. Sometimes I needed help with a lead into a new area or an introduction to people with a particular interest. Just asking a question in the right way was often enough.

Your success depends on your approach and how well you ask questions, particularly if your aim is to achieve a win/win outcome. It's always important to value and appreciate any help you are given and be prepared to return the favour. In my experience, people love to help if they can. When you ask for help in the right way, it makes people feel special. If they can't help you, or what's offered comes to nothing, that is fine too. My view is it costs nothing to ask and doing so could lead to a fantastic opportunity.

*'The only thing that stands between a man and what he wants from life is often merely the will to try it, and the faith to believe that it is possible.'*

RICHARD M. DEVOS

Other people have the potential to become your ambassadors as well as clients and good friends. One of my best clients came from a chance meeting at a local university. I was there to attend an event and because I was early, got chatting to the receptionist. We hit it off and she asked for my card. A few weeks later, I had a call from a senior director of an international organisation who was her personal friend.

If you take the time to invest in your relationships, not only will you be rewarded, you will stand out and be remembered. Your circle of influence depends on it.

# Eight

# BE BOLD

One of the most powerful lessons I have learnt, in business and from life, is that we have no idea what we are capable of achieving at any time. All we know for sure is what we have achieved until now. The future is ours to create and we will either define ourselves by what we have already done, or by what we still want to do. The first can stop us from even trying. The second opens the door to possibility. In that sense, we have a choice, but we can also choose to increase our chances of success.

Time and again throughout my life, I have been told that something cannot be done and I have always questioned why. Too often it is because someone else hasn't believed an outcome is possible, or they are unable to see a way to reach the goal. Yet I have learnt there are many ways to achieve a desired outcome. Our knowledge is so often limited by what we already know or expect to be true, yet new discoveries are continually being made. Why should we limit ourselves and not try? Much of what we learn about ourselves by trying is as valuable as the outcome we seek.

Thomas Edison, who made 1,000 attempts to achieve success with the light bulb, always claimed that he discovered 999 ways it didn't work before he hit the jackpot. He learnt from each attempt and used that feedback to shape the next one. It finally paid off and the simple light bulb transformed the lives of millions. History is peppered with similar stories. My personal philosophy is to find a way.

*'Whatever you can do, or dream you can do, begin it. Boldness has genius, power and magic in it.'*

JOHANN VON GOETHE

---

If you are serious about achieving success, and you have tried the usual routes and hit a wall, sometimes it pays to think outside the box. Focus on the outcome you want and be creative. Learn to trust your own wisdom, rather than rely solely on others. What is your gut instinct telling you? It is there for a reason, although many have forgotten how to listen. When your thoughts are focused on the outcome you want, rather than the difficulties the challenge presents, all kinds of possibilities will show up.

I hope this personal story will inspire and encourage you. Some years ago, my son Matthew left university with a 2:1 Honours Degree in Computer Science and a 1st for his dissertation. He had accumulated quite a few additional skills and plenty of work experience but, like many, struggled to find the career role he wanted. Eventually, he began a six-month contract providing IT support in the public sector while he continued to search for something more permanent and fulfilling.

Months went by without success. Finally, Matthew told me how frustrated he felt at being unable to get access to the right people. Everything was submitted online, competition was incredibly high and the recruitment process was soul-destroying. What he really wanted was to work in the City of London. He loved the idea of being part of the buzz of city life. When he described his vision, his face lit up and as he spoke, I had an idea.

At that time, we lived in a rural area with a main commuter line into London. Many properties in the locality were very expensive, so

42

I reasoned that the kind of people who could afford to live in them were probably decision-makers in the City.

**What if…** you were to stand on the London bound platform at the train station, with some sort of poster, stating exactly what you want, what you have to offer and invited people to ask for your CV?

**What if…** you were dressed in a smart suit, crisp white shirt and a good silk tie (borrowed from Dad), so that you absolutely looked the part?

And **what if…** you got up very early and were on the platform by 6am, to catch the decision-makers before you went on to work? (This one made him gasp.)

As Matthew listened, I saw he could visualise what I'd described and, to his credit, he agreed to give it a try. Very quickly, he created a brilliant, laminated A3 poster with a powerful message that stated exactly what he was looking for and what he had to offer.

It was a brave thing to do and took courage, determination and a leap of faith to take the risk. But it paid off. By 7.10am on the first day, all his CVs had gone. More were requested in electronic form, so that people could forward them on to their contacts, whilst others gave out their business cards. Without exception, everyone was encouraging, supportive and wanted to help. As interviews and job offers followed, I counselled Matthew to hold out for a role he really wanted. At the third attempt, a call came through from the Vice President of IT Europe of a high profile investment bank, inviting him for an interview later that same day. Two further interviews followed, along with practical tests to demonstrate ability and knowledge. By the time he met with HR, the offer was just a formality. Taking that action not only achieved his goal, but it led on to opportunities and experiences that he had never imagined in his wildest dreams.

So let's get focused here on what you want and how you can increase your chances of success:

- Begin by knowing your desired outcome. It has to be something that begins 'I want… '
- Find a way to get access to the decision makers. Who do you know who can help?
- Set yourself up to succeed. This is very important. You need to be well prepared, not just in what you say, but how you communicate your message. Communication is your currency of success.
- Be prepared to step out of your comfort zone. Having the right mindset and support makes all the difference. This is all part of your preparation.
- When you are fully prepared, take a leap of faith.

When you see yourself in a role, or have a specific outcome in mind, your goal becomes very clear. The challenge is to find a way to close the gap between where you are now and the outcome you want. Regardless of the goal, don't give up because you cannot see a way forward. If you limit yourself, based on what you have done or experienced until now, or on someone else's opinion of what is possible, you may never know what might have been. Instead, develop the tools, strategies and mindset you need to power your actions and support you in attaining your goal.

*'Be daring, be different, be impractical,*
*be anything that will assert integrity*
*of purpose and imaginative vision*
*against the play-it-safers,*
*the creatures of the commonplace,*
*the slaves of the ordinary.'*

SIR CECIL BEATON

## Exercise

Take some time to think about what you want and create a strategic plan of action.

**Q.** What bold action could you take to achieve the outcome you want?

**Q.** Based on what you've learnt, how can you set yourself up to succeed?

The world is changing so rapidly that none of us can be sure what the future holds. Why limit your vision now. It is all too easy to adopt other people's limiting beliefs about what is possible, because that means you don't have to put yourself on the line and find another way forward. What they mean is it wasn't possible for them. You have to decide for yourself what you want and create your own definition of success.

There is a belief in the existence of a glass ceiling for women. It is used to justify why there are not more women in top-level jobs or achieving success in a male-dominated industry, yet there are women who do. In spite of the very real challenges that exist for women, many have a can-do attitude. They think differently. They refuse to be limited by other people's beliefs; they live by their own. They accept that when you are at the forefront of change, there is always a price to pay, so they fight harder for what they want. They are prepared to learn from their mistakes and invest in themselves because they are determined to succeed.

> *'There is no glass ceiling.*
> *A manicured fist will smash*
> *it as well as any man's fist.'*
>
> HILARY DEVEY

Create a vision for yourself that both excites and scares you. Give it as much detail as you can and then build your plan. Break it down into clear actions. Identify the outcomes you want to achieve at each stage and include whatever you need to get there. Then, measure your progress continuously and refine your actions until you achieve the outcome you want. If you keep your desired outcome at the front of your mind, and you are committed and determined to succeed, you can change the game.

Part Two

# SELF-MASTERY

# Nine

# MINDSET

To achieve real success in life, you need to learn how to master yourself. Mindset is everything, because no matter what you face in life, you can choose your response. Developing your mindset to support rather than undermine you is essential for your professional and personal success. By being more aware, you can take control of your thoughts and responses, rather than allow them free reign over your life. It takes commitment, because too often we respond out of habit, but such conditioning can be changed.

The effort you invest and your willingness to challenge your own unhelpful thoughts and behaviours have the power to transform not only the way you feel about yourself, but the success you achieve.

Begin by knowing the outcome you want. How would your successful, future self think? What would that person believe about their abilities? What would their attitude be to the obstacles they face and how would they deal with them? Adopting the attitude of the person you need to become in order to achieve your goals is a powerful strategy that holds you to account. It not only changes your mindset, but it transforms the way you perform.

*'Your living is determined by the attitude you bring to life: not so much by what happens to you as by the way your mind looks at what happens.'*

LEWIS DUNNINGTON

Many people give up on themselves and what they want, because their thoughts and limiting beliefs sabotage their actions and prevent them from reaching their goals. Once you realise the only way you can be defeated is when you accept defeat, every challenge or failure becomes an opportunity to learn and grow. You can choose to give up, or you can see failure as feedback to help you become more courageous and effective. Fear and self-doubt are perfectly normal emotional responses, so acknowledge them. Then adopt a mindset of success and commit to overcoming those fears. In the process, you begin to master yourself.

**This is what happens:**

- With the right mindset, it's easier to move out of your comfort zone and manage change
- Your confidence increases and you develop more of a can-do attitude
- You take responsibility for the choices you make, based on the outcomes you want
- You start actively making decisions that shape the direction you want your life to take

This attitude stands out from the rest. No matter how able, most people play it safe and never truly fulfill their potential. Stepping up can be scary, but it is also exciting. If you have embraced the message of this book, I hope you are beginning to see yourself and all the possibilities available to you in a new light.

> *'Knowing others is intelligence;*
> *knowing yourself is true wisdom.*
> *Mastering others is strength;*
> *mastering yourself is true power.*
> *If you realise that you have enough,*
> *you are truly rich.'*
>
> LAO TZU

From personal experience and from working with clients, I know that we don't always realise how much we have been influenced by our upbringing, until something happens that causes us to question the root of our attitude and beliefs. When I was young, family life was very stressful. Just navigating every day was like walking on eggshells, waiting for the next explosion and its consequences. As I grew older, I became very clear about what I *didn't* want. The problem was, I had no idea how to create the outcomes I *did* want.

As children, we gain our sense of self and how to be from the influences in our environment, our culture and from those who care for us. People do the best they know how, based on their own knowledge, past experiences and learning, but they may not know how to give us what we need to live happy, confident and successful lives. Limiting attitudes, beliefs and behaviours are often passed down through generations, with ongoing consequences. As adults, we must take responsibility for our own lives, but we can only do that once we understand that we have a choice. Until we do, our lives will always be limited.

I recall clearly the day I realised I had a choice. At a business discussion, I had shared my views with a colleague about the need for a strong self-image as the foundation of real confidence. She asked me whether I had read Louise Hay's now famous book, *You Can Heal Your Life* and I resolved to buy a copy. Unlikely though it sounds, until I began to read her book, it had never occurred to me that I could choose my responses in all areas of life, even though I had done exactly that in a business context. I was used to thinking 'How can I… ?' in relation to my professional life. Everything I had achieved was because I was open to possibilities and learning, but on a personal level, I had wasted too much time trying to make sense of the many 'why's' in my early life. That perspective had kept me looking back on experiences beyond my control and things I couldn't change. In that light bulb moment, I realised I had a choice.

On that momentous day, I drew a line in the sand and began the journey to become who I wanted to be. My focus completely changed and I began to see myself and my life in a very different way. Instead of looking back, I focused on the present and what I needed to change for the woman I wanted to become and the life I wanted to live.

The first time I used this concept in a workshop, I took along a number of brown cardboard boxes in various sizes, ranging from tiny to huge. I ran a white line along the length of the room and invited the participants to choose the boxes that represented their challenges. I then asked them to stand on the line facing in the direction they felt best represented where they were in their lives. This meant facing forward, looking back or standing sideways on, for the present.

When everyone had chosen their boxes and were positioned on the white line, quite a few were looking back. One of the participants explained that the future seemed very scary, so she stayed facing outwards; another chose the biggest box of all. As she faced the future holding this huge box in front of her, she was completely hidden. I asked her who or what the box represented. 'All the men in my life,' she replied.

The way we look at our lives has a significant influence on the outcomes we achieve, as well as how we live through the choices we make. Being aware of your attitude and choosing only to accept thoughts that empower rather than undermine you is the first step in changing your mindset and developing your personal power.

> 'A great attitude does much more than turn on the lights in our worlds; it seems to magically connect us to all sorts of serendipitous opportunities that were somehow absent before we changed.'
>
> EARL NIGHTINGALE

Once you accept the importance of attitude, you can begin to master your thoughts. You become more mindful of your thoughts, the assumptions you make and what you expect. If you catch your own thoughts putting you down, you can cancel them and replace them with a positive message that supports the outcome you want.

In a different scenario, you may find yourself overreacting to something or someone because you are tired or stressed. Afterwards, you regret your response and turn on yourself. Rather than berate yourself, learn from the experience and accept that none of us are perfect. Make amends and then consider how you could have managed the situation in a more effective way, so that you are programming your mind for future incidents.

# Exercise

- Acknowledge any patterns or unhelpful behaviours that have become habits
- Consider ways to avoid the situation occurring, i.e. being over-tired or stressed
- Identify strategies you could you use in the future, if faced with a similar situation.
- Visualise yourself applying these new strategies
- Tell yourself that you have learnt from the experience and that you will do better next time
- Apologise, if possible, for the way you over-reacted, not for the issue
- Congratulate yourself on your willingness to learn

Developing a mindset of success means focusing on the outcomes you want, but unless you master your responses, you are at risk of self-sabotage. Become accountable. If you make a mistake, accept it and take positive steps to rectify the situation. If your over-reaction is with an employee or someone close, he or she will understand that making a mistake is okay, as long as you put it right and learn from the experience. The willingness to understand depends on the learning.

*'Don't be afraid if things seem difficult in the beginning. That's only the initial impression. The important thing is not to retreat; you have to master yourself.'*

OLGA KORBUT

Marilyn ran her business from home, but was constantly interrupted by her close family network. She loved them dearly, but they all assumed that because she was single and based at home, she was endlessly available to meet their needs. Their requests ranged from child-minding to running errands and generally being a constant support system in their lives. Pushed too far, Marilyn became resentful. When eventually she lost her temper and over-reacted, she was filled with remorse, turning the situation on herself. I discovered that the real problem was her lack of boundaries and her ineffective communication, not an unwillingness to help out. With greater awareness, some clear boundaries and better communication, Marilyn was able to transform the situation with her family and manage her business and personal commitments effectively.

Attitude matters. When you have the right mindset, your approach can transform the outcomes you achieve. In all areas of life, new results begin to show up fast. Mastering yourself means recognising you have the power to choose how you respond to the challenges you face. You have the ability, through determination, perseverance and hard work, to drive your own success and create the outcomes you want, rather than hope or wait for them to just happen. Once you know and apply that mindset, it transforms how you feel about yourself and your sense of personal power.

# Ten

# FEAR: THE FLIPSIDE OF EXCITEMENT

Everyone experiences fear. It is normal to feel anxious and even fearful at times. Fear seems to be part of the cycle of learning, a by-product of the unknown. As we face new challenges that take us out of our comfort zone and all that is familiar, we put ourselves on the line. Uncertain of the outcome, we understandably feel vulnerable.

The day I moved into my first flat was so exciting. Yet as the door closed and I was finally alone, a sudden wave of anxiety washed over me. My mind raced with 'what if's'. What would I do if a fuse blew? What if a pipe burst? How would I cope? I had absolutely no idea. It seems ridiculous now, but in those days there were no mobile phones, I had no landline and this was pre-internet. The area was new to me and if anything went wrong, all the responsibility was mine. Yet my fears were groundless, as they so often are.

Fear comes up when we are being stretched and forced out of our comfort zone. We experience varying degrees of panic, anxiety and sometimes outright fear when we feel unsure of our ground or vulnerable. This is compounded when we also lack the knowledge or experience to know that we can and will cope. In that moment of vulnerability, fear takes over. The greater the challenge, the more fearful we become.

When I taught my first Jafra class to a room full of strangers, I had no idea that in a few years' time I would be presenting with confidence to large audiences at regional and national meetings, with barely a second thought. I was so nervous that first night and immensely grateful for my longer length skirt because my knees were shaking so much. Interestingly, no one else seemed to notice or care. It was all going on in my head. The real issue that night was my lack of confidence and experience, not my ability to teach the class... and that was within my power to change.

We become fearful when we are dealing with the unknown, yet I have come to realise there is another side to fear. The flipside is excitement. When you embark on something new and unfamiliar, whatever that may be, it is inevitable you will face some level of anxiety, even fear. Yet you get through it and come out the other side. The more challenges you overcome, the stronger and more confident you feel in your ability to cope. I see it as building inner reserves of courage to make future experiences more manageable. With time, you discover that courage is not being without fear, as the late Susan Jeffers wrote. Instead, it is 'feeling the fear and doing it anyway'. That's real personal power.

On the journey to achieve your goals, there will be many experiences and your commitment will be sorely tested. I have asked myself more than once, 'Why am I putting myself through this?' when faced with a particularly challenging situation. The simple reason is, I refuse to be someone who doesn't try, even when the circumstances are daunting, because I know the joy and elation that accompanies any worthwhile and meaningful personal or professional challenge. I can only describe it as a feeling that anticipates the sense of achievement in the attempt. My thoughts are always, 'What if I can pull this off? Wouldn't that be amazing!' And then you find that you can and did. I have learnt that deep down we all want to shine, to make a difference, to find out who we really are at our best and what we are capable of achieving. The only thing that stops us is fear, and those imagined 'What ifs...'

*'Only those who risk going too far can possibly find out how far one can go.'*

T.S. ELIOT

In 2005, I was told I needed surgery for skin cancer in two places on my face. I'd had it before and knew it was probably caused by sun damage in my teens from the years I had lived in Spain. In those days, few people had been aware of the dangers posed by the sun. I'd had surgery during the first trimester of my pregnancy and, although upsetting at the time, it had been a simple procedure under local anaesthetic that left me with a small, barely noticeable scar on the side of my nose. This time, I was shocked to be told the procedure was far more invasive and no one was sure what the visual outcome would be. I admit to having been very scared. The surgery was planned for a month's time.

The day after I was given the prognosis, and whilst still trying to come to terms with the news, I received a call. I was invited to speak at an event at the London Stock Exchange with an anticipated attendance of up to 750 professional women. The event was two days before my surgery. Would I be interested?

As I held the phone, many things went through my mind. The prospect of speaking at the London Stock Exchange was both daunting and exciting. I'd never spoken to an audience of that size before, let alone for 30 minutes. Oh, and they wanted my presentation to be interactive with the audience.

I knew that I had to find the courage to go ahead with the surgery and, more importantly, deal with whatever followed. I reasoned that if I turned down this opportunity, no matter how daunting, I would always regret it, regardless of how things turned out. In that defining moment, I decided to use the courage I had to find for the surgery and direct my focus on the presentation. I took a leap of faith and said 'yes'.

> *'I have learned over the years that when one's mind is made up, this diminishes fear; knowing what must be done, does away with fear.'*
>
> ROSA PARKS

Over the course of the following month, I refused to think about the surgery and the 'what ifs...' Instead, I focused on all I needed to do to prepare for that presentation. On the day, it went exactly as I'd planned, except on arrival, I was advised that my presentation was also being shown on huge screens around the building. I preferred not to think about that and kept my focus on the audience in front of me. When the surgery took place two days later, I was still on a high. I had managed to reframe the fear into something positive to help me take on a challenge that was exciting and daunting, yet full of opportunity. It taught me a powerful lesson in managing fear. Thankfully, both events had successful outcomes.

Fear is a response, a state of mind that you can flip over, like a coin. On the other side you will find the challenge and with it an opportunity to grow. When you take on a challenge that really stretches you and makes you anxious or even afraid, you gain something of great importance. You learn how to master yourself.

Every time you are presented with an opportunity in life, you have a choice as to how you respond. You can use your fear to galvanise you on to greater things or you can become its victim. Either way, none of it is about what you are capable of doing or overcoming. It is all about choosing the right mindset and then preparing yourself for the challenge. Once you decide to conquer your fear, have a clear outcome in mind. Begin by knowing exactly what you want, even if the goal is to try. Then develop whatever tools or strategies you need to support you and increase your chances of success. Preparation is the key. Being well-prepared increases confidence, reduces anxiety and gets you ready for the challenge.

It may help to understand the root of your fear, so that it can be challenged. Many people's lives, including my own, have been influenced by difficult experiences at a time when they have been unprepared and ill-equipped to cope. These experiences can hold them back, creating limiting beliefs about what is possible. You may even have some of your own that come to mind. Unchallenged, fear becomes a powerful energy drainer that can limit your life and change who you are, but only with your consent.

> *'Fears are educated into us and can,*
> *if we wish, be educated out.'*
>
> KARL A. MENNINGER

Start by identifying the nature of your fear and notice where it comes from. Is it real or perceived? The acronym False Evidence Appearing Real is a useful measure. If you allow fear to have free reign in your life, you can drive yourself to distraction. Mastering your thoughts allows you take back your power. Focus instead on the outcome you want, prepare well and refuse to accept the 'what ifs'.

There are many ways to manage and overcome fear. Try noticing how it manifests in your body. Where do you find you react? Do you feel it in your gut? Does your voice rise? Do your hands begin to sweat or your knees shake? Notice the way your body reacts and take control. Begin with some long, slow breaths to calm your breathing and restore you to a more balanced state. Keep a bottle of Bach Rescue Remedy, a safe and effective, tried and tested flower remedy that comforts and reassures. Use it when anxiety threatens. Learn some simple meditation techniques or try finger point pressures to help you relax.

Begin by sitting or lying down and relaxing your shoulders. Using both hands, start with the index fingers and lightly press your thumbs to their pads. Hold for a minute or two before moving your thumb on to the next finger. As you focus your attention on each pressure point in turn, your mind will calm. This is a useful exercise to do in bed, when you want to sleep.

My personal favourite is a powerful mantra, repeating to myself over and again: 'I am a strong confident woman. I can do/handle this.' It calms mind and body and brings me back to where I want to be.

These are all powerful coping strategies that work. They can easily be adopted into your life to provide positive support whenever you feel anxious or uncertain. Rather than give away your power by reacting and turning to negative self-talk or unhelpful behaviour, take control of your fears and flip them over for the opportunity they present to master yourself.

Breaking the event or activity you fear into manageable steps, rather than dealing with it in one huge leap, is a great help. What are the individual steps you need to take – are each of these frightening on their own? Probably not. Remind yourself that you have experienced many firsts throughout your life and chances are you were scared or anxious before each one. Remember that first date? The sheer excitement of going out with someone helped you overcome your shyness and anxiety. What about your first day in a new job? You survived because although you were nervous, you were also excited. Fear needs to be kept in perspective. There are many things we learn to overcome in life that seem daunting at the time, but somehow we survive.

When you truly master yourself, you learn to manage fear. Use it to increase your personal power and propel you to even greater success. It is part of the journey to wisdom. As you take on new challenges, you learn to feel the fear, yet focus on the excitement of the challenge. Every small victory empowers you to greater success and prepares you for the person you were always meant to be.

## Exercise

1  Pin up your goal or your vision of success where you can see it every day to remind you of what you want
2  Be aware of any fears that come up and create empowering strategies to help you deal with them
3  Surround yourself with people who support and encourage you to be your best self
4  Adopt an empowering mantra that inspires and keeps you focused on your goal
5  Take control of your thoughts. Choose to accept only those that support and empower you

*'You gain strength, courage and confidence by every experience in which you really stop to look fear in the face.'*

ELEANOR ROOSEVELT

It is perfectly natural to want to feel safe and secure in life. Safety is a basic and fundamental human need, so we need to work with it. Yet too often, we are discouraged from pursuing our dreams or conditioned to hold back. Women, especially, are labelled as risk averse, yet how much of that is conditioning? There are many men who feel the same way, but this is rarely admitted and never discussed.

In an ever-changing world, where we rely on other people and material things to meet our needs, life offers no guarantees. Build your own personal power and develop the tools, strategies and mindset you need to support you. View any challenges as opportunities to test your courage and determination to succeed. Refuse to be a victim of fear, but instead someone who has learnt to manage it wisely, to achieve their goals. As your personal power increases, your business, career and every aspect of your life will be transformed.

# Eleven

## ENERGY DRAINERS

Some of the greatest causes of frustration and stress, leading to unhappiness and poor performance in your business or career, are the energy drainers that undermine wellbeing and quality of life. Energy drainers take many forms. They are the people you dread spending time with, the tasks you need to complete but never get round to, and the challenges you try to avoid. They are things you have learnt to tolerate and they niggle away, causing worry, frustration and unease. Without action, they continue to undermine your peace of mind, your performance and your success. Most damaging of all, they change how you feel about yourself.

Energy drainers have the power to disrupt your sleep, shorten your temper and affect your relationships. You recognise them as the knot in your stomach, the worry you try to ignore, or an irritation you prefer not to have. Sometimes they disappear into the background, forgotten for a while until something happens to remind you. Then they return to the fore, 'shoulding' on you for not being good enough, or taking action sooner. Either way, their presence causes stress and affects your performance, taking up valuable time and energy, until they are addressed.

On an emotional level, energy drainers leave us feeling tired and weary. They represent the Shoulds in our life, not the Wants, and their power to undermine can be far-reaching, unless we learn how to manage them effectively.

*'Problems call forth our courage and wisdom; indeed they create our courage and our wisdom. Problems are the cutting edge that distinguishes between success and failure. It is only because of problems that we grow mentally and spiritually.'*

M. SCOTT PECK

Energy drainers are anything or anyone that drains your mental, physical or emotional energy and causes stress and unhappiness, affecting the quality of your life. They make it impossible for you to be your best self until they are addressed, so why do we tolerate them?

We may have learnt not to make waves, to keep the peace at any cost or to put our own needs last. Perhaps we've been told we are selfish to want more and to accept that this is life. Sometimes, we don't even realise how much we have learnt to tolerate. Instead, we seek comfort in those things that make us feel better, self-medicating with food, too much alcohol, endless work, sex, drugs or shopping etc., and are afraid to speak up for fear of the consequences, real or perceived.

Making the decision to deal with your energy drainers is often the hardest part. Once you do, your focus and direction begins to change, along with your sense of personal power.

So – begin by identifying all the things you are tolerating. List them and devise a plan along with a timeframe. Some tasks are easy to address, whilst others take longer and may need regular pockets of time allocated to deal with them. If you need help, be sure to get it. Think of this as an investment in yourself that will pay dividends in happiness, wellbeing and performance, increasing the energy you have for your business or career. It is important to take back control rather than continue to give away your power.

Ellie originally contacted me for help with her performance at work, following a disappointing annual review. As we spoke, she identified a number of business and personal energy drainers that were undermining her confidence, affecting her performance and causing stress. Recently married, she was under pressure to move house, but saw no way this could happen anytime soon. She explained that her house was overloaded with years of accumulated stuff. The kitchen, sitting room and spare bedroom were particularly bad and had made it impossible for her and her husband to enjoy spending time at home. The clutter had become intolerable and was now beginning to affect their relationship.

One of the problems was that no one wanted to spend any time at the house, so weekends were frequently taken up with trips away. Ellie's demanding City job also meant that her time was limited. She had agreed to sort out the rooms and get the house ready for sale, but it felt like another pressure and she lacked the energy and motivation to begin.

As we tackled the professional issues, we also began to address her home environment. Based on small tasks with specific amounts of time allocated, we devised a plan to tackle the clutter. With this approach, the job became manageable and quickly produced lots of small wins that had a remarkable effect on her morale. Ellie's new enthusiasm and her measurable progress also had a positive effect on her husband. To her surprise, he began to help and over the following weeks, room after room was transformed. The energy in the house completely changed and it became somewhere people wanted to be. By the time Ellie brought in the decorators, she and her husband had decided to stay in the house and make it their family home.

*'Never measure the height of a mountain until you have reached the top. Then you will see how low it was.'*

DAG HAMMARSKJOLD

Here are some further examples of easily recognisable energy drainers. You may relate to them.

Cassie's experience reminded me of those family occasions when people feel obliged to invite relatives whose presence is felt before they even arrive. Regardless of how the relative behaved, Cassie had already created the stressful experience she dreaded, and it had all taken place in her head. By the time the relative showed up, anything she said or did was enough to cause tempers to fray.

In reality, the relative may not have been the easiest person to have around, but she had been given the power to create stress and disruption in Cassie's life. If the visit had been perceived and managed with a different mindset, it could have been an empowering experience rather than a huge energy drainer.

Simon's experience was different. He had a health concern, but like many people, found excuses to avoid getting it checked out. By the time he did something about it, his anxiety levels were so high that everything else in his life had been overshadowed, including his business. Yet when Simon finally went to the doctor, his worries proved unfounded. For months, he had wasted a great deal of energy on a perceived problem, rather than addressing the real issue. The consequences for his happiness, wellbeing and business performance were significant. Taking action to find out what you are dealing with is empowering, regardless of the outcome. It enables you to decide how best to respond from a position of strength, whilst doing nothing increases stress, undermines your wellbeing and every aspect of your life.

Denise had a familiar story to tell. She was overloaded and stressed, with a number of business and personal commitments that she had committed to address. A self-confessed people pleaser, she found it difficult to say anything she believed might upset others, so she struggled to cope with the ever-increasing demands on her time. She began to feel that her life was spiraling out of control. When I met her, Denise was miserable and losing all perspective.

Resentment, fear of letting people down, of not being good enough and, most of all, coming to terms with the realities of her life, had deeply undermined her confidence and self-belief. The seemingly endless demands had now become a massive energy drainer, undermining her business effectiveness and personal happiness. Denise needed to take back her power and regain her energy.

This involved creating some clear professional and personal boundaries, with strategies that supported her in her objectives. She needed to prioritise her current commitments and take action to address them, delegating where possible. Learning how to manage her time effectively, and being held accountable, helped Denise make measurable progress. With greater awareness, she began to manage her professional and personal life with new confidence.

Every task completed or challenge overcome, is a boost to your confidence, self-belief and personal power. Each small success leads on to the next. With a can-do attitude and tangible results, people around you will often pitch in to help. Best of all, you will feel energised, as though a weight has been lifted from your shoulders and wonder why it took you so long to act.

Addressing your energy drainers is an essential part of building your personal power, transforming your performance and increasing your business and life success. Start today and let me know how you get on at: www.inner-power.co.uk

# Twelve

# CHOOSE YOUR THOUGHTS

Many years ago, I realised that we can choose our thoughts and in the process, change our lives. Thoughts are a constant source of energy with the power to support or undermine our happiness and success. How we think can shape our lives. If you are in the habit of thinking the worst, that is what you are likely to attract into your life, but you also have the power to choose thoughts that expect the best and support you in attaining your goals.

Begin by noticing the kinds of thoughts you have. Is there a pattern? Do you have supportive and encouraging thoughts or are they full of scepticism and disbelief? Are they positive and empowering or the kinds of things you'd never say to your best friend? What messages are you giving yourself on a daily basis, and do they encourage or undermine you and the success you want to achieve?

*'We are what we think. All that we are arises with our thoughts. With our thoughts we make our world.'*

BUDDHA

Many damaging thoughts become habits. They are often repetitions of unhelpful messages that we read or heard in our formative years. Perhaps once designed to limit expectations, their message may have been passed down through generations in very different times. Yet unless they are challenged, such thoughts continue to undermine our happiness, potential and future success.

You may have noticed yourself repeating the same negative messages once said to you by a well-meaning teacher, parent or boss. If so, be sure to challenge and replace them with something positive, until you break the habit of putting yourself down. Every negative thought needs to be counteracted and then replaced with a positive one that reinforces and builds your confidence and self-belief. This is a powerful strategy for transforming your mindset.

Henry Ford said, 'Whether you think you can, or you think you can't, you are right.' Your thoughts are the preparation for what you expect and therefore what you attract. When you change your mindset to expect the best, your behaviour follows suit. You project an energy that attracts support and brings opportunities you never imagined. Dreams and ambitions that were once dismissed by others as impossible now have the potential to be realised. It all begins with the power of thought.

My son Matthew demonstrated this to me at 11 years old. Within weeks of moving up to secondary school, he was placed in Set 3 for Maths, which he believed was deeply unfair. He compared his own ability to that of friends and peers in Set 2 and considered the teachers had made a mistake. Concerned at his frustration, I talked him through his options. Clearly, his teachers believed he was better suited to the demands of Set 3. If he wanted to change their opinion, he would have to do the homework of Set 2 as well as his own to prove his ability. Whilst wishing to support my son, I also gently reminded him that he complained about the amount of homework he had to do already, but I promised to help him with his goal should he decide to go ahead. Then, I asked him to sleep on it.

The next morning, Matthew told me that he had decided to get into Set 1. He had thought it through and was determined to prove the teachers wrong. It was a defining moment for us both. Over the following months, he adopted a can-do attitude, and with sheer determination and a great deal of hard work, he achieved his goal within 18 months. It wasn't easy and in the beginning both he and I came under a great deal of pressure from the school, because the maths homework he submitted virtually doubled overnight. It took time to change attitudes, but when the teachers realised the decision was his and he would not be deterred, they began to acknowledge his progress and support him in his goal.

That experience had a profound effect, changing many attitudes, yet it is only one of countless stories in which people were unable to spot potential. They make judgements based on their experience or beliefs, which are often limited by what is known. Opinions can and do change. There are many factors that influence success and sometimes people get it wrong. One of the most famous tales of missed opportunity is the story of how in 1962 the Beatles were turned down by Dick Rowe of Decca. The official reason given was that guitar groups were on the way out.

We need to understand that other people's thoughts and beliefs are based on what they know and have experienced. They are not absolute truths. How you think and what you say to yourself can have a far greater influence on your life. You need to learn to trust your gut and make a commitment to shape your own success. There is much to learn about what is possible and if you never try, how will you ever find out how far you can go?

*'Impossible is just a big word thrown around by small men who find it easier to live in the world they've been given, than to explore the power they have to change it. Impossible is not a fact. It's an opinion. Impossible is not a declaration. It's a dare. Impossible is potential. Impossible is temporary. Impossible is nothing.'*

MUHAMMAD ALI

When you change your thoughts from 'I can't' to 'How can I?' you will notice the difference. That response to any given situation or experience will change the outcome. Thoughts really do matter. They have the power to influence the way you feel, the choices you make and the actions you take.

## Thoughts ➲ Behaviour ➲ Results

With greater awareness, we learn to make better choices. We realise that we have the power to choose the messages we accept and those we refuse. I compare it to being thrown a ball. When the ball is thrown, you are faced with a number of choices. You can catch it and hold on to it. You can catch it and throw it back, or you can choose to ignore the ball completely.

Unfortunately, the way we think is often the result of conditioning and habit. That would be useful if we were all encouraged and taught to be strong, confident and determined, but it can be self-destructive if the messages we learn are life-limiting or undermine our self-belief.

A high achieving client with low self-esteem recalled how, as a child, she had achieved an amazing 99% in an exam, yet her father wanted to know what went wrong. Like a pebble dropped in a pond, there are consequences from such early experiences that ripple out into our lives. They continue to shape our sense of self, unless we are willing to challenge them and take back our power.

Many years ago, at the beginning of my career in Jafra, I had a heckler at one of my very first classes. It was a successful class, with good sales and further bookings, but I came away with the woman's comments playing on my mind. By the time I spoke to my boss, I felt anything but successful. Marie was a wise and experienced leader, who had learnt a thing or two. When I related what had happened, she laughed and told me that the poor woman who had heckled me had probably spent the last few hours cleaning her oven, or perhaps she had rowed with her husband before leaving home. In all possibility, the woman arrived at my class desperate to vent her day on someone. That doesn't make it right, but her words changed my perspective. We have all had similar experiences, but they can only affect us if we let them. By taking them personally, we accept the ball we've been thrown and in doing so, give away our power.

So take notice of your thoughts and what comes up. Be aware of the power your thoughts have to influence how you feel and the choices you make. Challenge anything that is unhelpful and replace it with something that empowers you. The more you do it, the easier it becomes, and one day you will realise you have broken the habit.

As you notice your thoughts, you may discover that your automatic response is to think the worst or put yourself down, but how is that going to help you achieve the outcomes you want? Instead, catch the thought immediately and challenge it. Now follow it up with something you want to be true. Here's the process:

Original thought: 'I'm running late. I'm never going to make that train. I'm always late. Why can't I get my act together? What's wrong with me?'

Does that resonate? Of course, your last question will lead on to endless examples in support of the negative message, so stop right now. Challenge the thought and follow it up with something far more empowering. It goes something like this:

New thought: 'Cancel that. You know what? I'm doing just fine. Everything is under control and I'm on course to make that train. I prepared well and I'm making good time.'

When your thoughts become more empowering, you relax and feel in control. Tension makes everything more difficult, including the ability to think rationally. You also become more effective at what you do, which saves energy and time.

As you work towards your goals, look at every aspect of your life and ensure you have the support systems you need, to optimise your success. Your thoughts are just one part of your support system.

*'Nurture your mind with great thoughts, for you will never go any higher than you think.'*

BENJAMIN DISRAELI

Look closely at who and what influences the way you think. Imagine working alongside someone who only sees problems and spends all day pointing them out. That kind of daily influence on your life would soon have a negative effect on your performance and happiness. Your mindset would tune in to the negative frequency and in no time, you would find yourself focusing on all the problems in your own life. Many people feel the same way about newspapers and avoid listening to the news. If your mind is constantly subjected to a diet of doom and gloom, it's easy to imagine the world as a truly terrible place and become fearful and depressed. Again, you make a choice. Be aware of the influences in your life and whether they support your happiness, wellbeing and personal vision of success.

Negative thoughts will come up when you feel most vulnerable. A small voice sometimes seems determined to undermine your resolve and overwhelm you with self-doubt. This is when fear can take over. Such thoughts have no authority over you, unless you accept them, so notice and discard them. They are not worthy of you, or your vision of success. Challenge and replace them with something powerful and supportive. The more you do this, the more confident and empowered you will feel.

> ## 'Our greatest battles are with our own minds.'
>
> JAMESON FRANK

As you begin to recognise your own patterns of thought, it is really helpful to create a mantra, or surround yourself with supportive messages that reinforce the outcome you want. When a new challenge comes up, you will realise that your thinking has changed to 'What am I going to do about this?' rather than something negative. Master your thoughts and you will truly feel happy and empowered to achieve success in any area of your life, regardless of the challenges you face.

# Thirteen

## EMPOWERING BELIEFS

Beliefs are powerful drivers that influence the attitudes and behaviour of everyone. They can be supportive, inspirational and empowering, moving us to exceed our own expectations of what is possible, or they can hold us back and greatly limit our lives.

In times of challenge and adversity, empowering beliefs can make a significant difference to the outcome and level of success we achieve. Used consciously, they can increase our focus and determination, even when the odds are stacked against us.

Such belief also inspires confidence in others and reinforces our determination to achieve our goals. Most importantly of all, empowering beliefs change the way we think, transforming the energy we project, the opportunities we attract and our willingness to take risks.

Of course, beliefs are only part of the story. You still have to do the work, but a great belief helps you start from a place of strength. At their most effective, empowering beliefs open your mind to possibilities and influence the way you think, which helps you to recognise and embrace opportunities when presented. Rather like a great role model who has done it before, an empowering belief can inspire and drive you on to bigger things. It can help you master your fears and keep going no matter how daunting the challenge, empowering you to reach your goals.

> *'Create the highest, grandest vision*
> *possible for your life, because you*
> *become what you believe.'*

OPRAH WINFREY

---

My own philosophy of 'I can do this. I just need to find a way.' has helped me face and overcome many, many challenges. For the most part, I would begin with no idea of the 'how', just an absolute belief that somehow I would do it. It seems to me that the real challenge in life is not whether you can achieve your goals, which questions whether you are good enough, but how you can achieve them. That means you need to be creative, resourceful, determined and committed to action, rather than allow yourself to feel disempowered from anxiety and self-doubt.

Chris was a director in a male-dominated industry. She had worked with the MD for many years and knew him quite well. In recent months, he had become very stressed, often treating her with disrespect when their paths crossed at the company's weekly meetings. At first, whilst she was surprised and upset by his behaviour, Chris made allowances. She knew the MD had family issues and was under pressure. By the time we met, she had reached the point when she felt there was no alternative but to leave the company. Her encounters with the MD had deeply undermined Chris's confidence in her position and she needed some help to move forward.

I discovered that Chris really enjoyed her role, but found it difficult to assert herself. She lacked a strong, empowering belief about her right to be treated with respect. She also needed to set some clear boundaries and improve her communication skills. Once she had the right tools in place and we had developed a strategy, Chris was able to speak privately to the MD in a calm, clear and assertive manner about his attitude towards her. Faced with this reality check, the MD immediately apologised and went to great lengths to ensure she remained with the company. He admitted that he had allowed his personal circumstances to affect his attitude and behaviour at work.

Chris's success encouraged her to make further changes in her personal life. With support, she began to invest regularly in her own wellbeing and to recognise and challenge her own limiting beliefs. This had a positive influence on the way she was treated in all areas of her life.

> *'You have to believe in yourself, that's the secret. Even when I was in the orphanage, when I was roaming the street trying to find enough to eat, even then I thought of myself as the greatest actor in the world.'*
>
> CHARLIE CHAPLIN

There are many ways that beliefs touch our lives. Some influence the way we value ourselves. Other beliefs shape our views and expectations of the world around us. They all have the power to influence behaviour, even subliminally.

Michael was very stressed and wanted help to make the big life change he believed would resolve his situation. As we talked, I discovered he rarely got enough sleep and it was often interrupted with nightmares. Michael had come to believe that the only way to get off the treadmill of his life was to have a breakdown, and had seen this happen to a colleague some months earlier.

A highly successful senior director in his mid-forties, Michael worked long, 18-hour days. Without realising it, he had been driven by a belief that 'hard work never hurt anyone', taught him as a teenager by his father. Unfortunately, Michael had a number of health problems and living his life by that belief was actually causing him serious harm. Once we identified the unwitting root cause of the situation and challenged the belief, Michael became receptive to making some significant changes to the way he managed his professional life.

With a different perspective, he learnt to overcome his reluctance to delegate responsibility, which had greatly increased his workload. He also began to question and negotiate the time he allocated to meetings and, importantly, he learnt how to relax and have fun. Taking control of his working life put Michael in the driving seat and much to his surprise, his health, wellbeing and quality of life dramatically improved.

Beliefs that no longer serve us need to be challenged. They often originate from thoughtless, throwaway comments made by others during our formative years. Left unaddressed, they continue to affect self-esteem, undermine potential or as Michael discovered, impact our health, happiness and wellbeing. Whilst empowering beliefs provide support and encourage us to be the best we can be, limiting beliefs usually reflect some form of criticism or repression.

This has been one of the challenges women face within the workplace. Our beliefs shape the way we think and what we expect. In a working environment dominated by men, women traditionally were given supporting roles, rather than seen as leaders in their own right. The skills, confidence and assertiveness needed for leadership in the workplace were qualities primarily attributed to men. Any man who put himself forward and determinedly argued his case was generally admired and seen in positive terms, whereas a women who demonstrated the same skills, risked being labelled aggressive and difficult to work with. Those stereotypes still exist at times and need to continue to be challenged.

Much is about perception and changing the attitudes and expectations of both men and women. In the meantime, women need to step up, become more aware of, and take responsibility for, their own limiting beliefs, replacing them with positive and empowering messages that support their success. When they do, they amaze themselves.

> *'Be who you are meant to be and you will set the world on fire.'*
>
> SAINT CATHERINE OF SIENA

Sara was a bright, talented and ambitious young woman, yet she lacked the confidence and self-belief to go after what she really wanted in her career. Eventually, she decided to get help, which brought her to me. I learnt that she had failed to get into her first university of choice, which was also her father's preference, and this had undermined her belief that she was good enough. Sara's professional journey had nevertheless been quite successful and she was reasonably happy, but her doubts lingered on, holding her back.

As we worked through her energy drainers, Sara realised that her life path had taken her in a direction that she would never want to change. Her university had been the catalyst for meeting people who were very important to her and for the most part she had been both happy and successful. Then, a job opportunity came up with her first choice university. The interview was a revelation. She realised how limited she would have felt had she won a place there in an ethos so very different to the one in which she had thrived.

For years, Sara had held herself back in the belief that she wasn't good enough. It was based on a very limiting belief. With her new perspective, she realised how fortunate she had been. This insight transformed her thinking. Until then, Sara had lacked the confidence to apply for what she called her 'dream job', convinced she needed ten more years' experience. Now, she agreed to go for it. In the first round of applications, she heard nothing, but after two months a call came through to see if she was still interested. The organisation had looked again at the applications and this time Sara was selected. At her second interview, she was offered the job.

In this rapidly-changing world, anything is possible. People have more opportunities than ever before, but along with them are new challenges and, at times, impossibly high expectations and demands. To survive and thrive, you need to develop your personal power and have the confidence to define success on your own terms. That means knowing who you are and what you stand for, and realising you are at the centre of your own life, no matter how many hats you wear. Your beliefs about what is possible will be at the heart of the future you create for yourself and others. Therefore, adopt beliefs that will help you to achieve your goals and ensure they are in alignment with your values. A wonderful, empowering belief has the power to transform.

# Fourteen

## MAKING A CHOICE

Our choices shape the direction of our lives. We make them based on what we know, think and feel, but what happens when our choices fail to serve our best interests? They may be rooted in limiting beliefs or driven by unmet emotional needs, rather than our own inner wisdom.

Sometimes we precede our choices with 'I know I shouldn't but …' as we momentarily justify our behaviour. We know the difference, but driven by our emotions and with little thought for the consequences, we indulge ourselves with an impetuous reaction and give away our power. Such responses not only prevent us from achieving what we really want, but keep us rooted in bad habits and unhelpful behaviour that leaves us feeling weak, vulnerable and powerless to change. There are always consequences to those moments of indulgence, beyond what seems obvious at the time. Our happiness, self-esteem and what we really want are undermined by our desire for short-term comfort. Yet none of us are victims of our lives, unless we choose to be.

*'The chief cause of failure and unhappiness is trading what you want most for what you want now.'*

ZIG ZIGLAR

Faced with choices that have the power to sabotage your goals and undermine your success in life, the ability to master yourself can transform your results. With greater clarity and awareness, you can support yourself more effectively and achieve the outcomes you want. Of course, some choices are easy to make and present few challenges, but others have the power to throw you off course and entirely change your direction. Effective coping strategies not only keep you on track to achieve your goals, but increase your sense of personal power.

Few people take the time to fully understand the choices they make, and the potential consequences. They make assumptions, based on what they want, believe or hope to be true, rather than any reality. The same applies in our relationships. Our choice of partner, friends, colleagues and even the people we choose as clients, all have an influence on our lives and the way we feel about ourselves. We rarely think of our relationships in terms of shared values, or consider what's really important to us in the people who share our professional and personal lives. It's only when things go wrong and relationships change that we stop and question our choices and the decisions we made. In hindsight, we remember tiny moments of disquiet and pointlessly blame ourselves because we chose to ignore them at the time. Yet this is valuable feedback that we can use to improve our judgement, the questions we ask and the boundaries we set.

To understand and acknowledge who and what influences our lives and consequently make better, more informed choices, is hugely empowering. It is said that we become the sum total of the five people with whom we spend the most time, so if you apply that philosophy on a daily basis, consider who surrounds you in your life. Are they confident, positive and supportive people who really believe in you, or those who drain your energy, undermine your resolve and bring you down?

*'Keep away from small people who try to belittle your ambitions. Small people always do that, but the really great make you feel that you, too, can become great.'*

MARK TWAIN

Relationships that enrich your life will encourage you to learn and grow. They support you when you pursue your goals and are not threatened by your success. However, there are times when you may face a different scenario. If your choices have the potential to affect other people's lives, or the behaviour of someone close is causing you stress, you need to find a way to address the situation rather than allow it to continue.

It helps to be clear about your own boundaries and what is really important to you. Then begin an honest conversation and acknowledge the problem from your own perspective, rather than apportioning blame. State your vision of success and what you want. This sets the framework for the discussion. When you're done, be prepared to listen in return. It can make a real difference to the quality of your relationship and the way forward, with the potential to transform the support you receive, as a client of mine discovered.

Following a serious sports injury, Andrew had to give up his management role with a large financial organisation. In time, he started a business and decided to work from home to save costs. Unfortunately, with a growing family, space was limited. His wife's business was also home-based, so during the day Andrew began to use his young daughter's bedroom as an office. Unfortunately, he never thought to discuss it with her first. When his daughter began to react in some highly-challenging ways, Andrew struggled to maintain his focus on the business.

As we discussed the challenge he was facing, Andrew realised that he hadn't considered his six-year-old daughter's point of view at all. It was a wake-up call. Once he apologised and explained the choices he faced and what he wanted to achieve, his daughter understood and became very supportive. Because her father began treating her with respect and consideration, Andrew's daughter changed her attitude and was happy to share her bedroom to help her dad.

Whilst Andrew's situation was easily resolved, your vision of success may be one that bears little resemblance to those of the people around you. In some cases, your desire for success may be perceived as a rejection of shared experiences and values. It can lead to resentment or in its most passive form, a lack of support. Whatever the circumstances, this presents you with a different choice to make. Do you hold yourself back because of those relationships, or do you accept the differences, stay true to yourself and move forward? It may be time to re-evaluate, make some changes and create space for new relationships in your life. Not everything is meant to last or stay in its present form. That is the process of life. Sometimes we need to be willing to let go of the familiar and embrace new perspectives, new possibilities and new opportunities to fulfill our potential and become who we need to be, for the life that's waiting for us.

It is a challenge that affects many people's lives. Even when there is clear evidence that we need to change our behaviours or renegotiate our relationships, not just with others but also with ourselves, it can be daunting to take that first step.

*'Every decision you make – every decision – is not a decision about what to do. It's a decision about Who You Are. When you see this, when you understand it, everything changes. You begin to see life in a new way. All events, occurrences and situations turn into opportunities to do what you came here to do.'*

NEALE DONALD WALSCH

During the time I worked in the cosmetics industry, I knew many talented and beautiful women who always seemed to be on a diet. It became part of their shared identity, yet not one of these women ever permanently lost weight. They all saw the problem as one of diet, discipline and deprivation, which quite naturally made them want to resist. Yet the real problem was the way they saw themselves. That influenced the choices they made and contributed to their unhappiness with themselves. If they had truly wanted to lose weight and they had a big enough reason, they could have done, but they lacked a commitment to their own wellbeing that would have stopped the cycle of yo-yo dieting, so any success was short-lived.

When you are really serious about losing weight or achieving any goal because it's a 'must' rather than a 'nice to have', you avoid sabotaging your own success. You make a commitment to yourself (and your coach) and plan how you are going to achieve the results you want. Relying on motivation to keep you on track is pointless, especially when you know from past experience that it is short-lived. Success needs a different approach.

Look at the problem in a strategic way and identify all that you need to succeed. Become accountable and put effective strategies in place that support you because without them, you will give away your power whenever your emotional buttons are pressed. Changing your perspective will influence and shape the choices and actions you take. Begin by adopting a mind-set that is congruent with your goals and the outcomes you really want. Sometimes, people only alter their behaviour following a life-changing experience. They adopt a head in the sand attitude for years, until circumstances or events challenge their perspective and they are forced to face up to reality. As a coach, the most frequent response I hear from clients is 'I never thought of it like that before.'

When you change the way you look at an experience or any challenge, you have an opportunity to transform the situation. You can choose an empowered perspective, face up to the challenge and become stronger in the process, or see yourself as a victim and allow the experience to define your life. A victim mentality is always one that responds out of fear, and that can be changed. If you make the decision to take action, your success depends on having an effective strategy and the right support in place. Remember, if you are truly committed, the challenge is not whether you can achieve success, but how you can do it. Anything is possible if you are serious about your goals. You always have a choice.

# Fifteen

## BE HONEST

The decision to take control of your own life can seem an easy one to make, but in reality, it means digging deep. Usually precipitated by stress, unhappiness or a sense of helplessness, you reach the point when you decide enough is enough and know that something has to change. To move forward, you have to be willing to face your fears and be honest with yourself, which can be both a challenge and a relief. The hard truth is you can choose to be defined by your circumstances or painful life experiences and give them the power to continue to undermine your confidence, self-belief and happiness, or you learn how to create the life you want.

*'Self-acceptance comes from meeting life's challenges vigorously. Don't numb yourself to your trials and difficulties, nor build mental walls to exclude pain from your life. You will find peace not by trying to escape your problems, but by confronting them courageously. You will find peace not in denial, but in victory.'*

J. DONALD WALTERS

My client, Lucy, appeared to be bright and bubbly when we met, but admitted to me that she was deeply unhappy. She had had a passionate yet tumultuous marriage and three children with a man she described as the love of her life. Unexpectedly, he died when they were both still young. Time had passed and although she was now in a new relationship, Lucy was unable to come to terms with her loss. She constantly compared her present to the past and it prevented her from moving forward and being happy. Lucy had had bereavement counselling, seen a psychologist and had now decided to try coaching. Although she liked the idea of being helped, Lucy unconsciously used every tactic she could to avoid facing up to the truth. She made a few changes, but it was clear to me she was still holding back.

On our third call, I challenged her: 'Lucy, what are you going to do when coaching doesn't work?'

'What do you mean?' she asked.

'Well, you told me that bereavement counselling didn't work and that seeing a psychologist was a waste of time, so what are you going to do when coaching fails?' I replied.

There was total silence. Ten full minutes ticked by without a sound. Finally, Lucy spoke: 'Okay,' she said. 'So what do I need to do?'

Lucy was finally willing to confront the truth and be honest with herself. From that moment, she took control and within weeks had transformed her family life and become a happier, more confident person. She also came to realise that many of the people in her life were unintentionally helping to keep her locked in the past. By having some honest conversations with family and friends, and setting clear boundaries, Lucy ensured that she was supported in moving forward as she committed to the next stage of her life.

When you decide to face up to the truth of your life, who you are and what you have experienced, you accept that life isn't perfect for anyone, regardless of how it may seem at times. Instead you take responsibility to change those things within your power that make you feel less. You learn to trust your own judgement and to be who you really want to be, rather than what other people expect. You invest in what Stephen Covey called 'the emotional bank account', developing meaningful relationships with others, whether in business or your personal life. It changes outcomes. Such honesty is grounded in integrity. It is also the foundation for self-esteem and comes from a place of strength, giving you new choices based on right action.

One of the most powerful things I have found as a coach is that when I take on a new client, I explain that I will always be open and honest with them, but not necessarily tell them what they want to hear. I need to ensure they are okay with that before we go ahead, but clients greet it with relief. So few people are prepared to be straight with us and the higher you go in business, the harder it is to get honest, objective feedback.

Obviously, my role is to help people reach their professional and personal goals in life and part of that is working with them to overcome the challenges they face. Without honest feedback, that would be impossible. We all need to be listened to without judgement. A coach needs to understand where people are now, in order to help them move forward. That's more difficult to achieve with family and friends who are influenced by needs of their own that prevent them from being objective.

Poorly given or unrequested feedback may be misinterpreted, putting personal relationships at risk. Family and friends understandably want to avoid the risk of hurt feelings, but there are times when honesty is really useful. As Lucy found, it can help you to reach decisions that move you forward.

Like many people these days, when my client Jane married her husband, he already had a son. For some years, the boy had lived with his mother, only coming for occasional weekend visits to see his dad.

As he got older, the boy's relationship with his mother became more fraught and their rows led him to stay away from home. Mostly, he stayed with friends, but occasionally he began to sleep rough.

Jane's partner was deeply concerned and quite desperate to find a solution. Many hours were spent travelling the long distance between their respective homes to calm things down until a solution could be found, only for them to explode again. As a career woman without children of her own, Jane struggled with the disruption in their lives, yet felt that the obvious solution was for the boy to live with them. However, she confided to me that she had always struggled with feelings of jealousy towards the boy and had felt like the outsider when he came to visit.

Having an opportunity to talk openly about her feelings, without fear of judgement or pressure, was essential. Most of all, Jane needed honest feedback and strategic support to manage the situation. Through our coaching sessions, she was able to discuss her concerns and develop a new and truly empowering perspective. The boy came to live with them and although at first there were some minor challenges, they were addressed and overcome. Over the following months, as their individual and collective relationship strengthened, all their lives became richer and more fulfilling.

> *'No one is in control of your happiness but you; therefore, you have the power to change anything about yourself or your life that you want to change.'*
>
> BARBARA DEANGELIS

Making the decision to face up to those things you want to change and being willing to take action is the beginning of self-mastery. It means being clear about what is important to you and the person you want to become. Whether you need to develop new skills, change attitudes or break patterns of behaviour, begin by being honest with yourself first. The problems you try to avoid will continue to grow until in some way, they get your attention. Don't wait until there is a crisis in a relationship, a serious health issue or a major career or business challenge before you face the truth. The mirror test is a really good indicator. When you look in the mirror, do you like the person you see looking back at you? Are you happy with who you are? If not, there is work to do.

Being honest with yourself means getting real. It comes from a position of strength, rather than weakness and takes courage. It means you are ready to take responsibility for yourself and the life you want. You know the truth of what you are dealing with and can make informed choices about the actions you need to take. Such honesty empowers you and builds self-esteem. It is founded on integrity, authenticity and self-respect. In mastering your fear, you project a more confident and authentic message about who you are. You begin to be the person you were always meant to be and that's exciting.

# Sixteen

# MANAGE YOUR TIME

Learning how to manage your time effectively is essential if you are serious about achieving the business and life outcomes you want. You need to become super-skilled at managing distractions and stay focused on those things that will help you reach your goals. In other words, you have to master yourself.

At this point, listen for the voice making excuses and giving you all the reasons why managing your time is so hard. I completely understand. I know how difficult it can be to juggle all the balls and stay focused on what you want. It is so much easier to lose an hour of your working day chatting to a friend, checking your emails or getting lost in social media. Managing your time means having discipline and self-management when you don't feel like it, as well as when you do. The reality is that if you want better results, you have to make some tough choices. Those short-term indulgences are sabotaging the time you have to invest in your success.

If you have ever travelled, you know that a journey needs to be planned and time is part of the equation. There are always distractions that can take you off course and places where you could stop off along the way, but if you want to reach your destination in a limited time frame, you have to stay focused on where you are going. In the process, you learn to manage your time and make decisions that ensure you achieve the results you want. If you find you are setting goals, yet give away your valuable time by always putting other people's needs before your own, or notice you seek distractions to make yourself feel better, consider the reason. What is the fear that is holding you back?

Many of the most stressed people I've worked with struggled to manage their time. Their lives were out of balance and whilst in the short term they could cope, it is not a sustainable way to live. Overload is never the best way to improve performance. It leads to burnout, stress and all kinds of other consequences.

If you feel you are on a treadmill, you need a new approach. Prolonged stress is an indicator that something needs to change. Unfortunately, many people respond by working longer hours. To some, it implies they're trying harder but in the process, they become less effective. In their efforts to cope, they lose perspective.

Irene was a talented designer and a self-confessed perfectionist. She worked very long hours and when I met her, was extremely stressed. Her eating habits were erratic and the only time she made for herself was late at night. Irene had got into the habit of sitting at her computer until the early hours of the morning, justifying her behaviour as the only way to keep in touch with family and friends. She went to bed very late, had little sleep and woke every morning feeling exhausted. Her company had two areas of concern. They were responsible for the designer's wellbeing at work, and her excessive billed hours were a drain on the client's budget.

I worked with Irene to change her perspective and help her set some clear boundaries around the way she managed and prioritised her time. She also learnt how to communicate more effectively and take ownership of the design expectations undermining her confidence. As her working hours became more reasonable, Irene had time for other interests. With some much-needed balance in her life, she became happier and more effective in her role, which increased her value.

Take control and focus on the real priorities. Think about what is important in the big picture of your life, not just one small part. Then, learn the skills you need to manage your time well. That is within your power and it will become one of your most valuable assets. Your success is not dependent on how much time you have, but on how you choose to invest it. Everyone has the same number of hours in a day, so think of your time as a valuable commodity. In the process of learning how to manage it well, you will develop and hone skills that are valuable in other areas of life, like personal discipline, strategic thinking and the ability to plan ahead.

If you had to account for how you spend your day, what would you discover? How much of the time you use out of your 24 hours is a conscious choice, based on what is important to you and how much is wasted on distractions, trivia and things that in terms of your success really do not matter?

This is something my son learnt at around eleven years old. He would return from school and head straight for the kitchen, *en route* to the fridge. As he went by, he would automatically switch on the small TV, perched on the kitchen worktop. With food in hand, he would return to stand there for about 20 minutes, watching nothing in particular, before heading upstairs to do his homework. One day, when he was complaining about the time he finished, I reminded him that it was because he always started late and that set everything back. Of course it had never occurred to him until then that he'd been wasting his own time in front of the TV after school. With new awareness, he preferred to have the free time later in the evening, when he could watch something that mattered to him.

*'I wish I could stand on a busy corner,
hat in hand, and beg people to throw
me all their wasted hours.'*

BERNARD BERENSON

If you want to increase your effectiveness, it is essential to plan your time. Fifteen minutes of daily and weekly power planning means you become more focused and commit time to specific tasks that you can measure and progress. I recommend you look at your day or week as a whole and include as much detail as possible, to make your professional and personal life easier to manage. This kind of planning can take a while to become a habit, but it is well worth the effort. At first, you will probably underestimate how long everything takes, but you will notice the difference. Then, as you become more effective and get better results, power planning will become a valuable strategy, reducing stress and keeping your busy life on track. Your diary will keep you focused and help you avoid the distractions or demands that might otherwise leave you with little to show for your day.

An important part of managing your time is the ability to set clear boundaries, both for yourself and with others. If you feel that time just disappears meeting other people's needs, you may want to be more specific about the time you have available. Saying 'no' can seem a challenge at first, especially if you are prone to trying to please, but it can be managed with the help of your diary and a few well-prepared strategies.

Unexpected interruptions must always be managed. In my experience, people understand if you tell them you are in the middle of something and unable to speak right now. As an alternative to a message-answering service, you can always suggest an alternative time to call or agree to ring them back when you are free. It is better to have the time to devote your full attention to the conversation and stay on course, than lose a chunk of your day. Don't allow yourself to be sidetracked, unless you have made an informed choice and the issue is both important and urgent. Anything less will add to the pressure and the time you need to make up.

Paul was a partner in his company and worked in an open plan office. He found it very frustrating to be constantly interrupted by members of staff and really struggled to get through his own workload. Once he lost his train of thought, it took him a while to get back on track and return to the task in hand. This happened constantly and he had become both frustrated and disheartened.

First, we identified the nature of the interruptions and then, his specific needs to be able to do his own work. We also identified his preferred time of day when he knew he was most effective. This was a slot around 11am. Talking it through, we were able to come up with a simple solution that gave him uninterrupted time at his desk, for at least an hour every day. He presented the strategy to the rest of the office, along with an alternative source of support for anyone who needed immediate attention.

By communicating effectively with everyone and setting clear boundaries, Paul's problem was resolved. In fact, this approach worked so effectively, that word spread. Paul's strategy became widely adopted by many of his business contacts, who learnt of his Prime Time slot when they called.

## Exercise

1. What undermines your effective use of time? List everything.
2. When are you at your most productive?
3. What boundaries could you set, to support you in keeping that time for productive work?

**4** What further communication strategies do you need, to effectively manage your time?

**5** What do you need to say and to whom do you need to communicate, to create time for your goals?

Good preparation can transform your success. Begin with a plan that focuses on what is really important to you and allow some wriggle room to manage the time you allocate. Your plan provides you with a framework, not only for the tasks you need to accomplish, but how, when and what you need in place, to make your day and week run smoothly. These include anything that is relevant to help you perform at your best. It is often the small distractions that eat up your time and as a consequence, increase the stress.

> *'Time has a way of getting away from us, because we never have a grip on it during the day...'*
>
> DOUG FIREBAUGH

Be realistic about the time you need. Most people underestimate how long a task will take, but with greater awareness, you will be more effective. If time management is a significant problem, try keeping a record of how you use your time and identify anything that could be improved. If you need a reality check, consider your hourly rate and how much money you waste when you are tempted by distractions or allow yourself to be regularly interrupted by unwanted calls during your working day.

Of course, there are times when people have more work than is realistic, but that is an indication of ineffectiveness at some level. Overload is never the best way to maximise performance. Instead it causes stress, burnout and health problems. If you run a business and feel that you are on a treadmill, you need to change your approach. Rather than put yourself down, take control and focus on what really matters. Learn how to manage your time well and if you need it, get help. Time management is always within your power to improve and one of the most valuable skills you can learn.

When you master yourself, you learn to prioritise your time by recognising those things that are important and making better choices. Perhaps you want more time to do other things you enjoy, or time to exercise or spend with people you love. Make a conscious choice about the time you invest in watching TV. Don't allow it to be a time stealing habit that prevents you from having the present and future you want.

The most successful people in life have the same number of hours in a day as everyone else, so it makes sense to value your time and treat it with respect. Your success is not dependent on how much time you have, but how you choose to use it. In the process of managing your time well, you can hone and develop skills like personal discipline, strategic thinking, delegation and the ability to plan ahead. In every moment, you are making and acting on choices that shape your life, in exchange for your valuable time. Increase your personal power and make conscious choices that work for you. When you master your time, you change your world.

# Seventeen

# MASTER YOUR COMMUNICATION

Effective communication is far more than the sharing and receiving of information. Communication influences every part of people's lives. It shapes their relationships, the way they think and feel, what they believe or expect and inevitably, their professional and personal success. Much of the stress of daily life is rooted in the way people communicate. Yet effective communication is a skill that can be developed. With greater awareness, you make better choices and are more likely to achieve the outcomes you want.

Running a business or managing a demanding career is tough, especially if you are juggling family commitments. You need all the help you can get. Mastering the way you communicate, is one of the ways you can reduce stress and make your life or business work. All it takes is a little more thought at the outset... not always easy in the busyness of life.

Effective communication means ensuring the message you give out really is the one you want others to receive. That may seem obvious, but how many people take it for granted that others share the same understanding, insight and train of thought? They focus on themselves and what they want to say, rather than whether their message is received and clearly understood. Too often, language is vague and expectations misread, bringing consequences that add to the stress in people's lives. Whilst you have no control over how your message is interpreted, you are responsible for its communication and ensuring the receiver understands what you mean.

*'There are people who, instead of listening to what is being said to them, are already listening to what they are going to say themselves.'*

ALBERT GUINON

Communication can be a frustrating process. When people fail to communicate effectively, the consequences can be far reaching in both their professional and personal lives. Lack of awareness or a willingness to invest in improving personal skills means endless opportunities are missed. Relationships can be harmed or lost forever, workloads increase, adding to the pressure on limited resources, and businesses or individuals fail to perform at their best. In my work as a coach, many of the challenges clients face are related to communication. It has the power to undermine business performance and career progression, confidence and self-esteem and financial success. Poor communication increases stress levels, wastes potential and impacts on the happiness of everyone involved.

I was approached by a medium-sized company to coach a highly-talented project manager who had upset various members of staff and was behaving in what was considered an aggressive manner towards clients at meetings. When asked, the company made it clear to me that unless a solution was found, they would have no alternative but to terminate the project manager's employment.

I found the young man to be very personable, but quite arrogant. He came from a cultural background with a dominant macho culture and had a superior attitude. By his own admission, he could often be blunt and it was clear that he had a number of fixed beliefs that influenced his attitude and communication style. His admitted a lack of engagement at meetings and impatience with colleagues and clients. Before I could help him, I needed his agreement and commitment.

I began by asking him about his professional goals and what success would mean to him. He said he enjoyed his role and was keen to build a career with the company. It was important to him to be happy at work and be proud of what he achieved, but he was under pressure with a heavy workload and struggled to manage his time. He became frustrated when those he relied on failed to do what he asked.

'Can you describe the business you are in?' I asked him.

'I'm a designer,' he replied.

'Yes, that's what you do, but it's not the business you're in. Surely you are in the people business? Doesn't your success depend on your ability to connect with people, whether they are your clients, employers or colleagues? Aren't you selling you – your skills, your ability and your time every day, in return for your salary and position?'

He thought for a moment and replied, 'I hadn't thought of it like that before. How soon can we get started?'

As our weekly sessions progressed, he began to make significant changes that transformed his performance. He learnt to plan and manage his workload and time more effectively, which greatly reduced the stress. He learnt to communicate his instructions more clearly and ensure he was fully understood. This meant taking the time to think and being better organized. He also agreed to slow down his speech and be aware of his tone of voice.

With new insight and greater awareness, his attitude towards clients changed too. He became more attentive at meetings, more collaborative in phone calls and he learnt to use a 10-second delay strategy before giving a response.

Over the following weeks, he discovered that effective communication could achieve far better outcomes and began to revel in his ability to get results without the drama. He was happier in his job and became a valuable asset to the company, rather than a potential liability. In time, he was promoted to director level. The company saw his potential and were willing to invest in his talent, but it could have turned out differently if they had lost business from a disgruntled client, or members of staff had chosen to leave.

Too often in business, people make assumptions about roles and responsibilities that are not clearly defined or universally shared. The consequences cause unnecessary stress, reduce effectiveness and undermine business performance. Clarity and effective communication is essential.

One of the main causes of stress is a lack of boundaries, especially when running a business. This is part of the self-mastery toolkit. Unless you can clearly identify and communicate the outcomes you want, you may find yourself drawn into commitments you don't want, making agreements that are not in your best interests or endlessly procrastinating, all of which sabotage your success. Self-mastery means taking control and communicating well to achieve win/win. You may need to negotiate or delegate to reach the outcome you want, but if you are clear about your objectives and well prepared and confident in your approach, you will be in a stronger position to reach a mutually acceptable agreement. Preparation is key.

A client of mine, David, had an enormous workload. He was responsible for managing a number of senior people in various locations throughout the UK. He worked long hours, travelled great distances and was extremely stressed. Almost immediately, I discovered that David found it hard to have what he perceived as difficult conversations. He found negotiation to be a real challenge and struggled to trust others to do a job as well as he could himself. Instead, he strived to meet the demands and expectations of his boss, at the cost of his own health and wellbeing.

By changing his mindset and helping him develop and improve his communication skills, David was able to delegate some of his workload. His colleagues responded positively to this newfound trust and embraced the opportunity. Much to his surprise, David also discovered that his boss was perfectly happy when he suggested more effective ways to manage the workload. By taking control of the situation and delivering better, more effective solutions, he not only addressed the stress, but he increased his value to the organisation.

> *'To effectively communicate, we must realise that we are all different in the way we perceive the world and use this understanding as a guide to our communication with others.'*
>
> ANTHONY ROBBINS

Good communicators project authority when they speak. They are clear about what they want to say and well-paced and confident in their delivery. In business, there are numerous times when you need to present or speak in public and the level of your success depends on your credibility and the authority you project. Such opportunities are a great way to raise your profile and demonstrate expertise, but you need self-awareness and great preparation.

Effective communication, on the telephone or by email, is equally important. The first time I made a business call many years ago I was nervous, unprepared and totally ineffective. I waffled on, trying to make my point and acutely aware of how inept I sounded until I suddenly realised I was still speaking to the receptionist. When I was finally put through, I lost my nerve and hung up. The embarrassment forced me to master my fears and learn how to use the telephone effectively. I was determined never to put myself in that position again. It took thought and preparation, with lots of role-play and practice, before I reached the point when I could speak to anyone on the telephone clearly and with confidence. There is little point otherwise. Too often, we are faced with people who mumble or who are in such a rush to impart their message that you have to ask them to repeat their name and the information again. In business, that is a poor introduction and does not inspire confidence or credibility. Without a clear message effectively communicated, you lose all authority.

Your ability to communicate well in your professional life, whether you are giving a presentation, speaking up at a meeting or communicating one-to-one, can directly influence the success of your outcome. In business relationships, effective communication builds confidence, trust and credibility. It helps you stand out and ensures your message is heard. You have more influence and impact on those you want to reach.

Until now we have talked about communicating with others, but the most important area of effective communication is in the way you communicate with yourself. The one voice you hear for 24 hours a day is your own, and it has a direct impact on your self-worth, your happiness, wellbeing and overall success. What you say to yourself has the power to influence the choices you make, your actions, behaviour and the outcomes you achieve in both your professional and personal life. Therefore, be aware of the language you use and treat your self-talk as a potential support system you can draw on to help you achieve your vision of success. Anything less is self-sabotage.

Over the years, I have heard many clients describe the voice they hear when they feel challenged. Sometimes it is the voice of a critical parent or teacher. Others hear their own voice repeating unhelpful messages that have now become a habit. The origin is unimportant.

What really matters is how you choose to deal with that voice from now on.

Here are just some of the ideas clients have found useful. You may come up with a strategy of your own.

- Silence that voice in your ear with a big, pink gobstopper… the kind you used to find in an old-fashioned sweet shop.
- Visualise the person whose voice you hear. Now imagine them shrinking into the left-hand corner of your mind to become the size of a small toy. Give them a squeaky Mickey Mouse voice that makes you want to laugh. They will immediately lose their power to undermine.
- Imagine you have a waste paper basket with a firm lid. Now visualise transferring the voice to the bin and just put the lid on. All you will hear is a faint squeak.

These are easy ways to take control and master your negative self-talk. Make a commitment that you will never say anything to yourself again that you wouldn't say to your best friend. Learn how to communicate effectively with yourself by becoming aware of that negative voice and not giving it the power to undermine you. It is a choice you have to make if you are serious about your own success. Surround yourself with support systems that are designed to help you succeed. Challenge anything that does not encourage that goal, including the negative voice that can undermine your confidence, your courage and your self-belief. When you catch yourself going into victim mode, challenge the message and replace it with a positive statement that you want to be true.

At first, it will be like having a conversation with yourself, but as you practise and your conviction and confidence grow, the negative voice will recede. If you notice a habit of putting yourself down, get some help. The right kind of support can make all the difference when breaking a disempowering habit, whatever it may be.

Mastering your communication will greatly improve the outcomes in your professional and personal life, so be objective about how you communicate with yourself and others. Are you as effective as you want to be? If not, make a commitment to develop the mindset and skills you need to improve your results. Become more aware of how you communicate, so you can make better choices. Consider words or phrases that may have become an unhelpful habit, like overuse of the word 'sorry', or 'just', 'I'm only…' and 'to be honest'. These are all communication habits that subliminally undermine the impact of your message to others.

Becoming a great communicator is an investment in yourself and your performance. Effective communication builds confidence, transforms outcomes and increases your personal power.

# Eighteen

# BUILD YOUR CONFIDENCE MUSCLE

To achieve success in business and life, you need the confidence and self-belief to take risks so that you learn and grow. Every new challenge mastered increases your confidence and makes you stronger and better prepared for the next. No matter how confident you are, there will always be times when the unexpected happens and you suddenly feel vulnerable. Those external supports you may have relied on to boost your confidence will not be enough. True, unshakeable confidence comes from within. For that, you need to build the inner resources that give you confidence and self-belief and support you through any challenge. Here's why it matters…

Confidence influences:
- the choices you make in business
- how high you aim in your career
- any decisions related to your health
- how you manage your relationships
- your expectations around income
- the money you earn
- what you tolerate or are prepared to challenge
- how you feel about yourself

My own professional and personal experiences and all that I learnt from my work in Image taught me that real confidence comes from within. Whilst the right clothes and external image definitely boost confidence and improve your chances of success, they are only the outer layer. Without a strong foundation, that kind of confidence is an illusion. If you rely on it to feel good about yourself, or to support you in times of challenge, you become incredibly vulnerable.

Real confidence and self-worth comes from knowing who you are, feeling good about yourself and having the certainty, self-belief and inner resources to handle whatever comes your way. It means being clear about your values and having the confidence to make choices that support you, regardless of external pressures, time constraints or life limitations. At the heart of this kind of confidence is personal power.

Of course, there are times when you may temporarily be thrown off course by unexpected events, business challenges or the many demands of modern life. Self-doubt kicks in and unless challenged, it can undermine you further. Building the muscle of confidence and self-belief helps you respond from a place of strength, using obstacles as opportunities to learn and grow, rather than giving them the power to overwhelm.

With this mindset, you are better prepared to take action and more creative and resourceful in finding a way forward. In the process, your confidence increases, along with your resilience and personal power. Like any exercise, the more you work at it, the stronger and more confident you become. You may even appear taller, as Abi discovered.

Abi was in a business partnership that had greatly undermined her confidence. She had no doubts about her ability, talent or contribution but lacked the confidence to effectively challenge her partner's behaviour. She had tried to set boundaries around their different roles and wanted to be treated with professional respect and consideration, but struggled to make it happen. We began working together to address the situation and as Abi's confidence grew, a friend commented that she 'looked taller somehow.'

With a clear strategy aimed at achieving a win/win outcome, Abi called a meeting to address her concerns. Our coaching sessions had increased her awareness of the different partner contributions and areas of expertise in the business, so when she was faced with total resistance, Abi concluded that the partnership needed to be dissolved. With newfound confidence, she made the decision to set up on her own. Over the following weeks, she prepared well and on the day she launched her business, Abi had enough work to break even in her first year. Since then, her business has gone from strength to strength, along with her confidence and sense of personal power. She attracts high profile clients, has built an excellent reputation as an expert in her field and still walks tall.

> *'You gain strength, courage and*
> *confidence by every experience*
> *in which you really stop to look*
> *fear in the face.'*
>
> ELEANOR ROOSEVELT

Like most people, you may find that you have plenty of confidence in some areas of your life, but feel unsure or held back in others. It helps to recognise the specific times when you want or need more confidence and identify what would make the difference. Focus your energy on the actions you can take to achieve better outcomes.

When I agreed to speak at the London Stock Exchange, I made a point of visiting first to check out the auditorium and get a sense of the space. I also knew who my audience was likely to be and what they wanted, needed and expected to hear. That really helped.

Perhaps you find it hard to ask for what you want. That may well be a pattern in your life, holding you back and impacting at many levels, not least in your business or professional life. Begin by considering how prepared you are, before you go into any given situation and look at what you can do to increase your confidence and ensure a positive outcome. Consider:

- What you want or need to say
- Who you need to speak to and what they will want or need to know
- How you present the message through your approach and delivery
- Where you present it
- When is the best time

Check that you have all the information you need before you go ahead. You may find it helpful to practise, or fine-tune your communication skills with a run through. Your coach, a trusted friend and even a full-length mirror can help. Achieving a successful outcome is often about how you ask and whether you have the confidence to negotiate. If you are well-prepared, know exactly what you want and what you are willing to concede, you are more likely to state your case with confidence and increase your chances of success.

There are times when we are forced to deal with difficult scenarios that can undermine our confidence because we are ill-prepared. I once spent an afternoon with a teenager role-playing a challenging scenario she faced every Monday morning outside a maths classroom at school. Yet with some well-practised communication strategies, the teenager was able to manage the next replay with confidence, completely changing the dynamics.

At some level, you always know when someone oversteps the mark or behaves unreasonably, but you may not be prepared the first time it happens. Afterwards, you wish you'd had the confidence to challenge such behaviour. Adopting the right mindset and preparing yourself with some effective responses, should you ever be faced with that scenario again, not only increases your confidence, it has the potential to transform future outcomes.

Security determines how you handle your experiences. On hearing a man bad-mouth him, Buddha listened quietly and thoughtfully, before asking:

'If you offer something to a man and he refuses it, to whom does it belong? The abuse and vile names you offer me, I refuse to accept.'

Acceptance is a choice, not an obligation. You don't have to put up with anything that is thrown at you. Instead, develop the skills to manage your responses. Be clear about your boundaries and commit to making choices that support you. Perhaps you have noticed patterns in your own behaviour, or find yourself continually facing the same scenarios. Trying too hard to please others is a sign that your confidence needs some work, especially if you constantly compromise your own needs in favour of other people. From professional experience, such behaviour eventually leads to resentment and unhappiness. It affects the way you feel about yourself and undermines your confidence further, so stay true to yourself and look at where you may be giving away your power.

Whatever is holding you back, begin by addressing the things that undermine your confidence. Make it easy on yourself and break every challenge into small steps. What do you need to move forward? Your confidence will grow with every action you take, as you discover what's possible. Make the commitment. Become accountable. Learn from each new experience, until you master yourself. Confidence grows through self-discovery and by taking action. Start thinking like the confident person you want to become and act as if you already are, until it comes naturally. The more you practise, the more your confidence will increase.

True confidence radiates from within, so the way you treat yourself and are treated by others, has an impact on how you feel. You have no power over the way others choose to behave, but you can decide what you are prepared to tolerate. How you treat yourself matters too. It may mean learning to set boundaries and stick to them, taking care of your health and wellbeing or managing your self-talk. It may be creating an uplifting environment around you or investing in a new image so you look and feel good about yourself. These all send out a clear message that says 'I value myself'. It's a powerful message that inspires confidence in others, helps you achieve the results you want and leaves you feeling fabulous. Why would you settle for anything less?

At a time when so many women are known to lack confidence and self-esteem because of their weight, changing the way you see yourself and making an empowered choice can transform how you feel. It needs a change in perspective. Take your power back and decide for yourself what matters to you, rather than allow yourself to be judged or influenced by others. Treat yourself with respect in all things and make peace with who you are. That decision alone will increase the wisdom of the choices you make.

Part of valuing yourself and building the confidence muscle means learning to listen to and trust your gut. If something doesn't feel right, question why. Your gut instinct is like a sixth sense, there to guide and protect. Being confident means trusting yourself and drawing on your instincts to support you, regardless of the pressures around you, or the weight of authority or experience you are up against. Other people's knowledge and experience are important, but they have their limitations. Your body carries the wisdom of ages, so if your gut is trying to get your attention, have the confidence and self-belief to trust its wisdom and let it guide you to ask questions or think more about the decisions and actions you take.

Building your confidence muscle makes a significant difference to the way you feel, how you are treated and the business and personal results you get. It transforms outcomes in all areas of your life and begins with a change of mindset, sustained effort and a willingness to build the muscle.

Fear and self-doubt are part of the human condition, but you can refuse to be defined by them. With the right tools, strategies and mindset, your confidence will increase and anything becomes possible. Whatever you want to achieve, lack of confidence must never be the reason that holds you back. Use it to inspire your learning. Build your muscle of confidence and be who you were always meant to be. Your happiness and success depend on it.

## Part Three

# PERFORMANCE

# Nineteen

# IDENTIFY YOUR NEEDS

I became aware at quite a young age that support can make all the difference to the way we feel and the choices we make. It has the power to influence our thinking, drive our actions and change life outcomes. Talent, ability and hard work alone are not enough to ensure success. They are all important of course, but the right support really can transform our results. Without support, talent and ability can easily turn into frustration, unhappiness and wasted potential, an observation that had a profound effect on me as a child. It was some years later before I fully understood why support, or the lack of it, has such an influence on success.

When you run a business, the right support is essential. It influences your mindset and changes how you feel giving you the energy and confidence to take on new challenges and make your life and business work. Such support comes in many forms. It may be highly practical, providing the help you need to run your business effectively, manage the numerous demands of family life, or ensure you present your best self to the world. It can be emotional support, when you need an objective and confidential sounding board or some truly honest feedback.

Then, there are times we all experience, when you are under pressure and begin to doubt yourself. Support in the form of genuine encouragement and reassurance is invaluable. It transforms how you feel and gets you back on track. Finally, when everything gets too much, you need the kind of support that feeds the spirit, whatever that may be for you. This kind of support is great when your energy levels drop and you need some time out to do something uplifting or life affirming. It will leave you feeling inspired, renewed and ready for the next challenge.

In the context of success, the right kind of support enables you to not only do what you do best, but also to perform at your best. It is no surprise therefore, that successful business owners surround themselves with great people and clearly-identified support systems. They understand their time is valuable, so they work to their strengths and deliver outstanding results. When you run a business, knowing your own needs and limitations and ensuring you have the right support, is not an indulgence. It is a necessity. Women especially feel guilty about needing support out of fear of being judged, but it makes good business sense.

My client, Claire, was a successful property developer, but found it very stressful dealing with contractors. She related some of her experiences and it was clear she needed to find another way of managing her on-site work. I asked her whether she had considered employing a part-time clerk of works, perhaps someone who had retired and would enjoy working on small projects.

The role of a clerk of works is to maintain standards and represent a client's interests on a construction site. If Claire agreed, she would have a highly experienced construction professional who would deal with the contractors on her behalf.

She jumped at the idea and within a week, had found someone who was semi-retired and perfect for the role. It proved to be a win/win arrangement for them both. The clerk of works had bags of experience and became a great support to Claire and her business.

What do you need, to be the success you want to be? What would really make the difference, to help you achieve the outcomes you want? Be honest with yourself and identify what may be holding you back. Many of the reasons for business and personal stress, with its inevitable impact on performance, is due to overload. People try to do too much at once, or to meet the needs of too many people within a limited timeframe. The ability to delegate and set clear boundaries around how you manage your time and commitments has the power to transform your results. With the mental space to think and time to focus on your strengths, you become more creative and effective in what you deliver.

I once worked with a very talented yet frustrated client who sought a promotion to director level role. The promotion had eluded him, yet he believed he had proved himself many times over. Together, we looked at every aspect of his desired role and measured it against his current performance to identify the shortfalls.

By asking him to describe his typical working day, we were able to pinpoint a number of opportunities where he could raise his game. These included being more engaged with colleague concerns and going the extra mile, and having a more proactive approach to meetings. With thought and preparation, he could demonstrate leadership and contribute in ways that added real value.

Over the following weeks, he focused on the actions he could take, rather than his frustration. Greater self-awareness and a strategic plan increased his confidence. Every day, he consciously acted as if he was already in the senior role, taking clear responsibility and demonstrating his value to the company. At the next review after some very positive feedback, he was promoted to director level with a significant salary increase.

Great support is a key part of any success plan. No-one achieves success without people around them who can provide the support they need. It frees them to do what they do best. Part of your plan must include a fallback position with people who will step in and provide support in times of emergency. This kind of forward planning reduces stress and ensures you feel confident, organised and in control.

Consider your personal life. Can you count on the people around you to be there when you need them? Do they inspire and support your actions, or drain your energy? Are household chores equally shared, or is it mainly down to one person? Families have a role to play in each other's success. Usually, they all share a common goal, namely to live happy and successful lives but there are times when they may need to be reminded. So how do you create the family support you need to reduce stress, maintain relationships and make your life work?

Begin by identifying what needs to be done and when. Then be clear about the ideal outcome you want and hold a family meeting. I have found this works best around the table, perhaps over dinner when you have everyone's attention. Effective communication is the key to buy-in. Once you have outlined the position, start negotiating until you reach an agreement that is fair and reasonable. Never be afraid to expect children to contribute, regardless of age. Everyone can and must do their bit, and children gain immensely from sharing responsibility and seeing themselves as part of a team. You are aiming to achieve 'win/win', not 'they win/you lose', so be clear, stay calm and focus on your goal. If circumstances change, you can reassess.

When I met Karen, I discovered that she had given up her career to have a family some years earlier and her life now revolved around housework and chores. Her husband had a very successful job in the City, so she had no need to work, but she felt powerless to change the behaviour of her sons who, though lovely young men of 14 and 15, took her daily routine of cleaning up after them for granted. She was desperate to do something meaningful again with her life, but had lost confidence and struggled to find the time. Her despair was obvious.

Sometimes, when you're in the midst of a situation, you cannot see the patterns that have led to the outcomes you face. After we began working together, it very quickly became apparent to Karen that there was another way of looking at the situation. She realised that rather than doing her best for her boys, she was actually limiting them.

I worked with Karen to increase her confidence and help her become more assertive. She learnt how to ask for what she wanted and be taken seriously. In no time, these two young men were not only picking up their laundry, but ironing their own shirts too. They impressed her further by offering to make dinner one night a week each, which gave her more time to focus on studying for a new career opportunity. So impressed was her husband with the changes in his wife and sons, he decided to follow suit. He also signed up for a coach-training course, to increase his own professional effectiveness with his team.

> *'The most common way people*
> *give up their power is by thinking*
> *they don't have any.'*
>
> ALICE WALKER

The ability to ask for what you want and get a positive outcome is a learned skill, and the way you ask is as important as what you ask for. It means being assertive, rather than passive or aggressive, and aiming for a win/win outcome.

Many women are conditioned to put themselves last and often feel selfish when they don't, yet men too can feel unheard and hold themselves back. Of course there are times when it is both necessary and appropriate to put other people first, but when taking the back seat becomes a way of life, it is a consequence of the way you think and of your past conditioning. You cannot perform at your best, if you do not value yourself. Instead, you are more likely to experience stress, frustration and resentment. So learn how to ask for what you want and be specific. If you cannot achieve the outcome you want, use it as an opportunity to learn, improve and try again. Keep your ideal outcome in mind and learn how to ask in a way that people will buy into, so that everyone wins.

It helps to develop a circle of people around you, who want you to succeed. They will offer the encouragement, recognition and emotional hug we all sometimes need. In moments of self-doubt or when you are faced with a daunting challenge, these are the people who will not allow you to put yourself down or give up on your dream. Instead, they will remind you of your best self, what you have already achieved and how far you have come. That kind of support is essential when you are striving for success.

One of the most powerful and effective ways to encourage people is through recognition. Soon after I began working for Jafra, cards would arrive almost on a daily basis acknowledging my achievements; whilst in the greater scheme of things my early victories were relatively small, they represented progress. Surprised and a little bemused at first, I came to look forward to those cards, sent by my Manager and Regional Director. They were a form of recognition and I had never experienced anything like that before. I came to realise that many of the women I worked with felt the same way. Of course, such recognition was actively encouraged by the company because it inspired us to greater things, increasing the company's sales and growth, but so what? We benefitted too. Personal recognition was an acknowledgement that our achievements were valued and appreciated.

Genuine recognition is a powerful way to reinforce the positives and increase confidence and self-worth. It takes many forms but the effect can be far reaching. Few people receive meaningful recognition in their lives, so it is important to acknowledge your own achievements too. You may be the only one who knows what it has taken you to reach your goal, but that is all the more reason to mark your success in some way. Acknowledge and celebrate what you have achieved and how far you have come. Not only does it make you feel good, it reinforces the effort you made and encourages you to keep moving forward.

Sharing success and acknowledging support, especially through some form of celebration, creates memories and makes a real difference in life. Apart from reinforcing relationships, it increases everyone's understanding of the demands and commitments on your time. We all need to know that our efforts are appreciated. One client discovered that his small daughter blossomed, when thanked for her help and support during a particularly challenging time with his business. Until then, it had never occurred to him to say anything.

Relationships deepen when people feel valued and appreciated, so no matter how busy you are, make time to celebrate your achievements and share the success. The right support can transform your results.

# Twenty

# YOUR GREATEST ASSET

Extreme self-care is at the heart of peak performance, yet few business owners or career professionals factor their own wellbeing into their success plan. Instead, most people take themselves for granted. They assume their performance is a given and that they will always have the energy, resilience and drive they need to achieve their current and future goals. They rarely question whether they are performing at their best, or consider the big picture, namely that they are at the centre of everything they do and therefore their greatest asset.

Yet performance relies on more than ability or talent. Performance is influenced by the way you feel – energy levels, wellbeing, mindset, confidence and self-belief. When you are tired, stressed, overloaded or unhappy, energy levels drop and performance suffers. Over time, unless this is addressed, it becomes a downward spiral.

Just for a moment, imagine you are the proud owner of a beautiful and expensive high-performance car, essential to the success and smooth running of your business or career. How would you treat it? In all probability, you would make time to keep it in tip-top condition to ensure it performs at its best. You would use premium grade fuel to maintain its high performance and of course, it would naturally be serviced on a regular basis to maximise your investment.

Extreme self-care means applying the same principles to yourself, not as a quick fix or an indulgence, but as a way of travelling through life. Your body needs to support you throughout your journey, but that can easily be forgotten when you are under pressure. Wellbeing has to be part of your vision of success. If you are unwell, your quality of life is compromised and you cannot perform at your best. Yet when you feel fantastic, your results are very different. Energy levels increase, you project great vibes and undoubtedly attract new opportunities into your life. Vitality is essential to performance, quality of life and the success you achieve, so if you are serious about your goals, begin by investing in yourself and your own performance. It has the power to transform your business success, your career opportunities and the outcomes in your personal life. Why would you settle for anything less?

Ned, one of my clients, struggled with mornings. By his own admission, he never really became productive until around 11am. I discovered that he always skipped breakfast and depended on copious amounts of coffee to kick start the day. Colleagues found him irritable and at times, even aggressive, but Ned was also ambitious, which is the reason we began working together. Addressing his performance, I began by persuading him to try a different approach. He agreed to start eating breakfast, cut down on the coffee and make some changes to his diet. Within a week, Ned reported a difference in the way he felt. The early morning irritability disappeared and his energy levels increased.

Wellbeing relies on the fuel we put into our bodies to maintain energy levels and keep us in an optimum state of health. That works well when the foods we consume provide for our nutritional needs, but many do little more than temporarily appease hunger or feed a craving for something to make us feel better. As creatures of habit, we tend to buy and eat the same foods week after week, often with little awareness of the impact on our health and wellbeing until something goes wrong. Good nutrition increases energy levels and transforms the way we look and feel. It builds nutritional foundations that support our body's needs, so that we can deal with all the physical and emotional demands and ongoing changes throughout our lives. Improving your diet now is an investment in your present and future health, your wellbeing and long-term performance.

One of the challenges we all face today is how to fit exercise into our lives. For some the gym is ideal, but for others, including me, it is one of the most boring places to be. Over the years, I've coached many people who struggle with their fitness and the challenge of finding time to exercise. Some enjoy classes, but are often too tired by the end of a long working day. Others have unpredictable working hours that make it difficult to regularly attend.

Yet you can make a real difference to your health and wellbeing simply by being mindful and using your body whenever you can. Consider ways you can increase the activity in your life and then commit to doing so wherever possible, until it becomes a habit. Find things you enjoy doing, like walking, dancing or swimming. These all feed the spirit and offer some regular time out, whilst providing the vital physical effort needed to maintain good health and fitness. Think of it as an investment in your performance. If you also make it to a class, that's even better. The goal is to become more active every day and to make movement a way of life, because you and your body are in this for the long haul.

Here are some of the ways I've found to make exercise part of daily life:

- Use the stairs whenever you possibly can, rather than take the lift or escalator. Make it a personal challenge and just do it.
- Try walking at a brisk pace, rather than a stroll, at least for some of the time. Aim for 30 minutes a day
- Avoid the tube/bus or get off before your stop, so you can walk part of the way

- Find time every day to play music that makes you have to get up and dance and do it for 20 minutes or more. My favourite time is when I'm making dinner, but if you work from home, this could become part of your early morning or lunchtime routine. It's a daily investment in joyfulness.
- Commit to a daily stretching routine that keeps you flexible. If you don't enjoy the gym, try using hand-weights on alternate days to keep your arms in great shape. This is so easy, you could do it whilst watching TV and best of all, it really works.

Note: Do make sure you have proper instruction before you begin.

Making time to take care of yourself gives you a sense of wellbeing. It is one of the ways you can feed your spirit and feel better immediately. It is a necessity, not an indulgence.

Isabelle, a financial director in her early forties had a boss who was something of a bully. He often intimidated his employees and with little support at home, Isabelle's confidence had gradually diminished. When we began working together, we discussed her options, including some immediate changes that would make a difference to her wellbeing. One of them, aimed at improving her working environment, had an unexpected impact on both Isabelle and those around her.

On her way to work one morning, Isabelle bought some flowers for her desk. She thought nothing more of it but as the day wore on, she noticed people treating her differently. They seemed to be paying her more attention when she spoke and even her boss's attitude softened. Finally, a colleague asked about the flowers and Isabelle replied truthfully that she had bought them to brighten her office. The colleague was clearly unconvinced and in that moment, Isabelle realised that people assumed she had an admirer. It was a small thing, but it gave Isabelle the confidence boost she needed to begin to make significant changes in her professional and personal life.

Extreme self-care is really about how you treat yourself and the impact that has on your performance, happiness and wellbeing. It addresses things that have an influence on your energy, including your environment. The Chinese call this Feng Shui, the Law of Energy. If you live or work in an environment that feels good, it has a positive effect on your performance and wellbeing, but the reverse is also true.

Some of the challenges my clients have needed to address that have added to the stress in their lives include overloaded desks, disorganised paperwork, piles of filing, newspapers or magazines, as well as general clutter. These are all symptoms of the way you treat yourself and they become real energy drainers that undermine your performance. It is essential to your success and wellbeing to take control and create an uplifting environment that supports you, rather than one that diminishes your self-worth by dragging you down.

Katherine made little time for her own needs and with a demanding business, had seriously neglected herself. Although professionally successful, she told me she was deeply unhappy with her life. She worked seven days a week, had no time for herself and felt that every day was spent preparing to go into battle. The idea of taking time out for regular hair appointments or to buy herself some new clothes was something she had always viewed as an indulgence. Katherine's busy life and lack of planning also meant that she often forgot to eat. I had noticed how thin she was when we first met. Now she admitted that getting enough sleep was also a problem. Clearly, her self-neglect was having an effect on her health and wellbeing, as well as undermining her confidence and performance.

Taking a holistic approach, I began by changing Katherine's mindset. We developed some strategies to help her manage her time more effectively and redefined her vision of success. Then, with the help of a nutritionist, I encouraged Katherine to find out what her body needed to get back to an optimum state of health. Within a week, her sleep patterns began to improve. When she discovered that I have regular appointments with my own lovely hairdresser, whom I see as part of my personal support system, she began to feel more comfortable about booking her own. If you are in a professional role, good grooming is essential.

Katherine also made time to buy herself some new clothes and began to enjoy her life again. With the right support and a willingness to make her life and business work, Katherine got her life back on track. It transformed the way she felt about herself, increased the energy she projected and helped her rediscover how fabulous she could feel again. She saw it as defining success on her own terms.

The way you think has a real impact on the actions you take. Changing your mindset and putting strategies in place that support the outcomes you want, will transform your results. Practising extreme self-care is about valuing yourself, so that others do too. Look at all aspects of your life and identify any areas that need attention. Consider where you might be losing energy and ways you can increase your happiness and wellbeing. By taking good care of yourself, you will be stronger and in better shape, both for your business and to support others. Remember, you are your greatest asset. If you are serious about reaching your goals, you must invest in yourself.

## Twenty-One

# THE IMAGE OF SUCCESS

Until now, much of this book has focused on changing the way you think about what is possible and how it can be achieved. In your business or professional life, any drive for success means learning to see failure or rejection as an opportunity to learn and grow, but that can be hard to do. We tend to take challenges personally and it's easy to lose perspective, especially when our sense of identity is so closely aligned to our business or role.

It helps to mentally detach yourself from your personal emotions, and wear your CEO hat for business. Whilst currently you may be the only employee, that professional role carries a set of expectations that you can strive to live up to. As CEO, your job is to focus on what you can do to overcome challenges and lead the company forward, not to take them personally.

Similarly, if you are career building, think of yourself as your own business manager. Any challenges you face must be viewed as opportunities to learn and grow. Develop your knowledge and skills, find ways to overcome obstacles and become outstanding in your role. Rather than take rejection or failure personally, use it as feedback to help you step up. This small shift in perspective can change the way you manage failure or rejection. Taking it personally will limit you, but if you see these challenges as useful if unwanted feedback, they can help you to raise your game.

*'Leadership and learning are*
*indispensable to each other.'*

JOHN F. KENNEDY

To increase your professional success, identify what you want to be known for. Your business must reflect that identity from the outset. For example, if you want to be known for delivering excellence, project that in all that you do. Every aspect of your business will then be about demonstrating your vision and walking your talk in the most outstanding way. If you aspire to a high level role, take responsibility and develop a leadership mindset, so that others see your potential.

In reality, you are your brand. What you deliver is what you will be known for. So take time to evaluate every aspect of your business and ensure that what you project is congruent, authentic and irresistible to the audience you want to reach. In a nutshell, you have to walk your talk.

Everything about you, as well as what you say and do, is an opportunity to stand out from your competitors with a message that can positively influence others. It changes how you are perceived and how you see yourself. For example, would you trust someone to make you money, if they looked shabby and poorly groomed? How much confidence would you have in a fellow professional, if they were disorganised and always late? What if they drank excessively at business networking events or were inappropriately dressed? They may well deliver the professional services and care you need, but would you be willing to take the risk? Rightly or wrongly, impressions really do influence the judgements we make and the opportunities we attract.

Shortly after joining a successful design practice, a well-dressed architect I worked with was invited by one of the Partners to attend a meeting with a newly-acquired business client. Purely based on how he was dressed, the architect was taken for the senior person. The businessman assumed that the man in the suit had the authority. The Partner, who was more of a creative and used to dressing in casual attire, had not considered his image in the context of heading a business meeting with someone from a very different background.

Lack of self-awareness in a business context can greatly undermine credibility and authority. At professional networking events, I have seen women with flowers in their hair or wearing clothes or jewellery more suited to a party. I have been introduced to businessmen whose lack of personal grooming or love of garlic-laden food is the main message you receive. To be taken seriously in business, you need to create an impression that gets you noticed and remembered for the right reasons.

The rights and wrongs of pre-judgement are irrelevant in the face of reality. Everyone makes choices based on perception, so the message you project needs to be congruent with your goals and vision of success. One of the ways you can do this is to maximise your credibility through the impression you make. Dress for success and be congruent in your image. Consider whether the way you present yourself is designed to project authority, credibility and attract the kinds of opportunities you want. Does your image reflect well on the decision makers and those in positions of authority, or the people who might want to hire, promote or support you?

Only the very rich or successful can get away with not making an effort in business. Dress appropriately for your audience and role so that others feel comfortable, and always look professional. The impression you create will increase your credibility and authority and help you stand out for the right reasons. Aim to be accessible and approachable, yet always at your professional best.

In my Jafra days, looking professional and well-groomed gave me credibility and opened many doors. I was frequently invited to give presentations or take part in large, organised events with other associated businesses. It was easy to reach my ideal clients, the professional women who had the means to invest in themselves but often lacked time to shop. Looking the part mattered, but it was also important not to alienate those women who attended one of my classes in someone's home. They may have arrived after a stressful day caring for young children, or a long commute from work. Everyone needed to feel comfortable and at ease, so they could relax and enjoy the evening, without feeling less in any way.

I soon learnt that simply removing my jacket once I'd met everyone made a difference. When seating was tight and there were limited chairs, I joined those who sat on the floor. It helped to remove any real or perceived barriers in a sometimes-crowded sitting room and worked well for building rapport.

Dressing appropriately makes a difference, even if you work from home. A client noticed that on the days she worked from her office at home, she became easily distracted and was less engaged. The baggy T-shirt and shorts she had begun to wear during the summer months influenced her attitude. When she changed her dress to smart casuals, she became more focused and productive.

The way we dress influences how we feel, what we project about ourselves and the opportunities we're likely to attract. It also helps others to imagine us fitting in to their business environment. This was essential when my son stood at the London bound station, seeking a role in the City. He needed potential employers to imagine him successfully fitting in to their organisation. Had he not looked the part, it is unlikely he would have attracted the interest shown or the opportunities that followed.

However, there is more to image than just the way you dress. Years ago, when I began working with ambitious professionals who needed an edge to increase their success, I came to realise the importance of self-image. A strong, confident image has to come from within. How you feel about yourself, influences the confidence and self-belief you project. It shows up in your physiology and through the choices you make.

Truly confident people carry themselves in a different way. They generally walk tall and have good posture. They make eye contact easily and treat themselves and others with courtesy and respect. Much can be done to change the way we feel, by becoming more aware of how we use our bodies and what we project.

## Try this simple exercise:

- Stand in front of a full-length mirror and notice your posture.
- Now, stand tall and imagine yourself touching the ceiling with the top of your head. Notice the difference.
- Without losing your height, broaden your shoulders and try to get them to touch the walls of the room, either side of you. Take a deep breath, relax the tension in your neck and smile.
- Notice how different you look in the mirror and how you feel. Your body is taking up more space, your chin is lifted and you are looking straight ahead.

Practised every day, this exercise can make you more aware of how you carry yourself and how easily you can begin to change the way you feel. It is a great exercise for anyone who wants to feel more confident before entering a room, or when faced with a challenging situation. It is also especially powerful when taught to children or young people who lack confidence, because it provides them with a visual image of the change in their bodies when they stand tall.

When you lack confidence or self-worth, you become vulnerable to external pressures that can further undermine how you feel about yourself. It may be the physical changes of aging, or the inevitable challenges we all face in life, such as dealing with loss, relationship break-up, divorce, ill-health, economic uncertainty and career or business challenges. With strong inner resources and a greater awareness of your personal power, you are better able to manage change and find new and exciting ways forward.

Personal power comes from a strong self-image. Think about a time when you excelled at something and were surprised and amazed at what you achieved, or a time when you faced a daunting challenge and doubted your ability to come out the other side. At first, you wondered how you were going to cope, but looking back, realise that you found the strength, courage and inner resources needed. Your success and willingness to rise to the challenge was the result of the choices you made.

Knowing that you have these inner resources gives you confidence in yourself. You begin to understand that your power comes from within and is about the choices you make. It is where your real strength lies, rather than in external things that can be lost or taken from you. Personal power means you have the confidence and self-belief to face life's challenges and focus on the opportunities they present, rather than allow them to define you and make you a victim.

I've known many people who have been truly devastated by business or life events and the direction their lives have taken. Without the inner resources from a strong sense of self to help them cope, they have turned to medication, alcohol, food or other means to ease their pain, all of which have added to their problems. Whilst there are times when anti-depressants are useful, for many people they are a sticking plaster, not the solution.

Much of modern life seems to be driving people to rely more than ever before, on getting their needs met in material ways that give them the illusion of self-worth. Our celebrity culture, many aspects of the media and the general direction of our lives has created unrealistic expectations where the focus is on external image – how you look, what you have and the lifestyle you live. Little seems to be about who you are and why it is so important to develop the personal qualities, strengths and character traits that support real happiness, success and quality of life. These are part of our internal image. Such over-dependence on everything external makes people very vulnerable to change or loss and does nothing to encourage empowerment or personal responsibility.

A strong, confident self-image is the foundation for success. If you want to change your outcomes, develop the inner resources that enable you to be your best self, with the personal power to handle whatever comes your way. Be willing to get into the driving seat of your own life and go after what you want with courage and confidence. You have the power to make it happen.

# Twenty-Two

# BE A GAME CHANGER

Are you ready now to step up and amaze yourself? Are you clear about what you want? Have you drawn the line in the sand and decided to take control? If you are now thinking of yourself as CEO of your business and life, you are in the right mindset. Your future cannot be left to chance. You have the power to transform your outcomes by taking control and turning your vision into reality. You would not have come this far unless you were serious, so regardless of the challenges you currently face, adopt a can-do attitude and start building your plan.

Success begins with the right mindset, so focus on the outcome you want and adopt a strategic approach that will deliver measurable results. Develop whatever support systems you need to help you reach your goals and surround yourself with people who share your values, vision and mindset for success. The right people around you can transform your results. Once you decide on a course of action, be accountable for what you say you will do. You need to walk your talk to be authentic and have credibility. Talk without action keeps your vision of success in the realm of dreams and you want measurable results in both your business and life.

If you have ever worked with a coach, you will know that one of the great advantages in the relationship is being held to account. A good coach will not allow you to let yourself down. Their purpose is to help you achieve your goals and discover how amazing you can be, so you live up to your potential. That means ensuring you take responsibility for what you say you will do. The bigger the goal, the greater the challenge and commitment required, so if you struggle with procrastination or want outstanding results, get the right support and be accountable. When you take action, you learn to overcome your fears and limitations, grow in confidence and achieve your goals. Action delivers results, whereas procrastination keeps you stuck.

Running a business, or working towards any goal is always a challenge. It requires that you dig deep and have the discipline and determination to keep going, even when times get tough. Maintaining the right mindset is essential. When you have a meaningful and worthwhile goal, your commitment and determination to succeed becomes a driving force that inspires confidence in others and builds a momentum of its own. You attract opportunities that you may never have considered, are faced with challenges you may not have anticipated and in the process, you start to become who you need to be for the success you want.

Women are known for holding back in business or the workplace because they lack the confidence or self-belief to go after what they really want. They doubt their worthiness or ability to cope and there are numerous reasons for this. Yet I have always found this is more an issue of mindset than ability and it is something that can also apply to men. The challenges faced when you put yourself forward mean taking a risk, and the more you do it, the more confident you will feel in your ability to handle the challenge. Good preparation and the right support can transform your success.

There are countless opportunities to really step up and demonstrate your worth, regardless of the outcome. People buy people and you may impress someone enough to think of you when the next opportunity presents itself. Your showcase is in the presentation. If you are well prepared and have the right mindset, just taking on the challenge and giving it your best shot increases confidence and brings valuable insight. Not going after something you want because of self-doubt always leads to regret. Such decisions usually come from a limited perspective, which prevents you fully considering the opportunity and all that can be gained, regardless of the outcome. It is always within your power to be your best self, to prepare well and stand out, so take a step back and consider the big picture. You may just change your mind.

> *'It's a sad day when you find out that it's not accident or time or fortune but just yourself that kept things from you.'*
>
> WILLIAM HELLMAN

One of the challenges often faced as you work towards your goals is that life with all its demands can take over. Compare this to the different responsibilities of leadership and management, or the need to work on your business, as well as in it. Both are important, but one drives the actions of the other. In your role as CEO, and especially if you are running a small or medium-sized business, you need the ability to stay focused on your vision whilst delivering on the detail. It is a different perspective and it will influence the decisions and choices you make.

Running a small business means wearing many hats and at times, these can be in conflict. By identifying the different roles you play, you become more aware of the challenges this can present and your priorities in the wider context of success. Where relationships overlap, there is always potential for conflict, so setting clear boundaries and negotiating to reach an agreement is essential. All businesses benefit from having well-thought-out contracts, including those where a life partner or other family member plays a supporting role, perhaps helping with accounts, IT or social media.

What begins as a loving act to help you with the business can easily develop into an area of conflict that spills into your personal relationship. As CEO, you need to take ownership and be in control, with direct access to all aspects of your business, not just in those areas where you have expertise. This is not an issue of trust, but of taking responsibility. Consider the consequences if for any reason something went wrong and you had no control. In a SWOT analysis (Strengths, Weaknesses, Opportunities and Threats), you would be vulnerable and your business at risk.

When my client, Libby, set up in business, her husband agreed to take on the role of unpaid company secretary, dealing with the day-to-day invoices and accounts. It made good business sense to suggest they draw up a contract that clearly defined expectations and responsibilities from the outset, to ensure there was no ambiguity. Libby's husband was delighted and in total agreement.

Many potentially stressful situations where differences of opinion carry over into personal relationships can be avoided by ensuring that people know where they stand and by reaching prior agreement about the expectations and limitations of their role. Whilst it is normal to have a contract when employing people, few business owners think of it when they start out and are reliant on a partner for practical help or support. As CEO, your ability to consider the bigger picture and plan accordingly, not only protects your business but also your relationships as you grow.

*'Management is doing things right; leadership is doing the right things. Management is efficiency in climbing the ladder of success; leadership determines whether the ladder is leaning against the right wall.'*

PETER DRUCKER

Leadership principles apply equally in your personal life. The wife of one of my business clients miscarried their first child. Understandably, they were both upset, but my client was also deeply concerned for his distraught wife and told me he dreaded the due date. Clearly, this was a stressful time for both of them and whilst he had a great deal of support and understanding, his anxiety was having an impact at work.

I realised he needed help to see the situation in a new and more empowering light – one that focused on what could be in the future rather than what was lost. By changing his perspective, my client was able to help his wife make peace with the experience and focus on looking forward. A few months later he told me they were now anticipating a new due date, and in time he became the proud father of a healthy baby boy.

I share this story because it is a powerful reminder that unexpected events happen, but the right mindset can transform your outcomes, both in business and your personal life. Whatever challenges you face whether personal or professional, sometimes you have to take the lead for a bigger purpose. Life is like a roller coaster ride and your happiness and success depend greatly on your ability to manage its challenges and stay focused on what you want.

This same client transformed his department by example. When we began working together, he had a clear vision of what he wanted to achieve, but too often was caught up in the day-to-day demands of management to be really effective and reach his goals. Initially, his greatest challenge was managing his own time and prioritising business demands according to importance. As his awareness increased and he became a more focused and effective leader, he reported that others were following his example in the way they communicated with their teams and managed their workloads. Everyone's performance improved, the project managers delivered better results and the department became noticeably more productive.

As CEO, you are responsible for turning your vision into reality, not by working harder but changing the way you think about what is possible and adopting an approach that really works. By sharing your vision of success and developing the potential of others, you can often achieve outstanding results. This applies in business and your personal life. If your goal is to increase your success and feel confident and empowered, stop seeing problems as a challenge and instead see the challenges as opportunities to help you step up, stand out and discover your best self.

My son was the first in our family to go away to university and he started with two big goals. He wanted the best possible degree to give him real career opportunities in life, and he wanted to finish university without any debt. What began as an idea, became a possibility that turned into reality. This is how it happened.

When Matthew finished his A-levels, he wanted a break from education so decided to defer for a year. Rather than take a gap year, he was keen to work. He still had his part-time job in a supermarket on Friday nights and Sundays, but wanted to use his experience with computers.

An opportunity came up with a local company and he was offered a full-time role. To keep his options open, I raised the idea that if he continued with the weekend job and saved his full-time earnings over the following months, he would have a lump sum towards university. If that appealed, we were happy to continue supporting him.

At that time, we had friends in their thirties who were still paying off their student loans long before the dramatic increase in fees, so we had seen how student debt can impact on family life.

My suggestion was well-received and as his savings began to accumulate, I started to wonder whether it was possible to finish university without any debt. If so, how could it be done?

*'I believe life is a series of near misses. A lot of what we ascribe to luck is not luck at all. It's seizing the day and accepting responsibility for your future. It's seeing what other people don't see. And pursuing that vision.'*

HOWARD SCHULTZ

Over the following months, we devised a plan. It began with identifying the specifics like tuition fees, accommodation costs, basic living expenses including food, course books, stationery and a social budget. This gave us an idea of the annual costs and timeframes and meant we could plan ahead. We looked at ways to cut the costs, especially with books and travel and how to get the best return on his savings. We also considered the skills Matthew needed to learn, if he was to manage on a tight budget. These included learning how to cook simple, nutritious meals, how to shop wisely for groceries, how to barter and how to stick to a budget. Each month, we would visit him, laden with groceries and home-cooked frozen meals that would save him time and money and offer support.

At the supermarket, he discovered that a company transfer policy meant he could continue to work in a store near his university, without having to re-apply for a job. The shifts could fit in with his university sessions and offer the flexibility he needed. This was great news and gave Matthew an ongoing source of income each term.

Like the best of plans, ours was very detailed. It required regular monitoring and adjustment, plus a great deal of commitment and hard work. It wasn't easy but it paid off. The day after Matthew graduated from university, he repaid his student loan in full. What surprised me though, was that none of the students he encountered whilst there, had even considered they had a choice. Some treated their student loans as a windfall and others just accepted the debt as the price you pay for going to university. Years on, how many are still paying the price?

Whatever outcomes you want for your business or your life, it is within your power to achieve your goals if you are serious about what you want. Build your personal power and discover what is possible. Too many people give up when faced with life's challenges, without ever finding out how amazing they can be. They quote numerous reasons why they are up against it, as justification for giving up on what they want. How many times have you done the same? The right mindset has the power to transform your outcomes, so make a commitment to yourself that you are worthy of your vision of success. Learn to make better choices, respond differently, invest in the skills you need and build support systems that make a real difference to your success. Focus on the outcome you want and be the game changer in your own life. You have the power to create success on your own terms, so what's stopping you?

# THE NEXT STEP

To celebrate the launch of 'Game Changer' and to help you start changing the game in your own professional or personal life, contact me for a FREE, no obligation consultation and book your FREE 30-minute Confidence Building coaching session, based on the principles of personal empowerment in this book. All sessions are in the strictest confidence.

I hope Game Changer has inspired you to take control and start turning your vision of success into reality. If you would like to know more about the Game Changer Coaching Programmes and how they transform confidence and increase business and personal success, email me now at: gamechanger@inner-power.co.uk

Whatever is holding you back, the adventure begins the minute you decide to change the game. So take the next step now and get in touch at: gamechanger@inner-power.co.uk

# INDEX OF EXERCISES

# ACKNOWLEDGEMENTS

Thank you to all my clients, who over the years have put their trust in me and without whom this book would never have been written. It has been a joy to work with each and every one of you.

To my many mentors and teachers whose influence has challenged my thinking and helped me realise my own direction.

To Lucy my publisher, for her patience and understanding.

Special thanks to Debbie Stenning, Lou Walker, Chris James, Pam Moran and Julian Donnelly for giving up their time to read and provide invaluable feedback on my early manuscript.

# THE AUTHOR

Linda Everett is a business and executive coach, working with business owners, CEO's and career professionals. In 2002 she founded Inner Power, combining her experience in business with her skills in professional and personal development and long-term interest in the psychology of performance. She specialises in Leadership Development, Confidence Building and Performance and through her coaching programmes, has successfully transformed the lives and businesses of countless professionals.

Linda's interest in the psychology of performance began in the 1980's, whilst building her business in direct sales cosmetics. Developing potential was fundamental to the growth of her business and led to invaluable experience in business management, people development, leadership and goal attainment. Within a few years, her business had grown to nine branches throughout the southeast.

Highly skilled at moving people forward, whether in growing their business, standing out in their career or improving their personal life, Linda Everett has a wealth of experience in overcoming the challenges that affect performance, undermine self-esteem and limit professional or personal success. Her own life experiences have given her great insight and understanding, along with an holistic yet pragmatic approach to performance that helps clients turn their frustration into phenomenal results.

Linda can be contacted by e-mail: info@inner-power.co.uk
Or through her website: www.inner-power.co.uk
Connect with her on Linkedin: www.linkedin.com/in/lindaeverett
Follow her on Twitter: www.twitter.com/ArmednFab

www.ingramcontent.com/pod-product-compliance
Lightning Source LLC
Chambersburg PA
CBHW070544090426
42735CB00013B/3064